The Manager's IT Handbook
A Layman's Guide to Information Technology

By **Brendan F. Hemingway**

Chief Medical Information Officer, Coyote Labs

Second Edition (February 2018)

Copyright © 2018 Brendan F. Hemingway

All rights reserved. No part of this book may be reproduced in any form without permission in writing from the publisher, except by a reviewer, who may quote short passages within a book review.

ISBN 978-1986415750 / 1986415759

Printed in the United States of America

Cow and Calf Publishing
5 Spring Road
Branford, CT 06405

This publication is designed to provide information in regard to the subject matter covered. It is sold with the understanding that the publisher and the author are not engaged to render legal, accounting or other professional services. If legal advice or other expert assistance is required, the services of a competent professional should be sought.

Table of Contents

Preface - *Totally Rewritten*   12

Part I - *Background*   13

Chapter 1 - *About This Book*   14
What Do We Mean By 'IT'?   14
IT Organizations   15
Why Read This Book?   15
Why Write This Book?   16
  My Qualifications   17
Examples   18
Let's Break It Down   18
  Simple IT Model   18

Chapter 2 - *Abstraction & IT*   21
What 'Abstraction' Means Here   21
  Abstraction Pros   21
  Abstraction Cons   22
  On Balance   22
Example: The Cloud   22
Levels of Abstraction   23
  Layered Architecture   23

Chapter 3 - *Sympathy For Tech Support*   25
Culture Clash   25

Anatomy of Mutually Unsatisfying Tech Support	26
Reasons To Pity Tech Support	27
Complexity	27
Compartmentalization	28
Sometimes There Is No Answer	29
An Example from Real Life	30
Video Call Failure	30
Understanding For Tech Support	32
(Sometimes Just A Jerk)	32

Part II - *Hardware: Getting Concrete*   34

Chapter 4 - *Traditional Computers*	35
The Basic Overview from Chapter 1	35
Layers of Hardware	35
Peripherals	36
The Typical Traditional Computer	36
The Glories of System Software	36
Application Software	37
Getting Specific	38
So What Makes A Server?	38
So What Makes A Desktop?	39
So What Makes A Laptop?	40
Chapter 5 - *Nontraditional Computing Devices*	41
Sample Nontraditional Computers	41
The Smart Phone	42
Tablets	43

Networked Printers	44
BYOD To Work	44
Marketing & Packaging	45
Repeater	45
Extender	46
Wireless Access Point (WAP)	46
Protocol Analyzer	46

Chapter 6 - *Networking*   48

Layered Architecture of Networks	48
Some More Detail	48
Transport Layer	48
Network Interface	49
Network Protocol: IP	49
LAN vs WAN vs WLAN	51
Directing Traffic	52
Assigning IP Addresses	53
Static IP Addresses	53
Dynamic IP Addresses: DHCP	53
Dynamic Name Service (DNS)	54
Video Call Example Revisited	55
The Cloud and the Network	56

Part III - *Abstract Concepts*   57

Chapter 7 - *Data*   58

Files & Directories	58
File Systems	58

Directory Attributes　59
　　Directory Trees, aka Paths　60
Why Data Issues Arise　61
Common Kinds of Data　61
Images　61
Documents　62
　Web Pages & Images　62
Spreadsheets　62
Databases　62

Chapter 8 - *Computer Security*　64
Practical Matters　64
　Common Attacks　64
　Guidelines　65
Textbook Definition　66
　Dark Security Secret #1　67
　Dark Security Secret #2　67
Physical Security　67
Network Security　67
App Security　67
　Malware　68
Data Security (Encryption)　68
Privacy & Snooping　68
Tools Are Neutral, People Are Not　68
　Examples　68
All About Policy After All　69

Chapter 9 - *Virtualization*　70

How It Works	70
Brain In A Box	71
Layered Architecture of a VM	71
Why Virtualization?	72
Economy of Scale	72
Uptime (aka Availability)	72
Legacy App Support	73
Virtualization and Users	73
Virtualization and the Cloud	74

Part IV - *System Administration*   75

Chapter 10 - *System Administration*	76
Sysadmin Areas of Responsibility	76
Uptime / Downtime	76
Configuration	76
Backup & Recovery	78
Preventive Maintenance	78
Security	79
User Credentials	79
Occupational Hazard	79
Nanny Sysadmin	79
Scheduling PM	79
Roles & Policies	80
Chapter 11 - *Backup & Recovery*	81
Kinds Of Failure	81
Backup Trade Offs	82

Kinds of Backup	82
Recovery	83
What Can Go Wrong	83
Kinds of Recovery	84

Chapter 12 - *Users, Printers, Servers & Shares* — 85

Users	85
Printers	86
Servers	87
File Servers	87
Shares	87
Database Servers	87
Web Servers	87

Part V - *Development & Deployment*   89

Chapter 13 - *Programming Language Overview* — 90

What This Chapter Is Not	90
Basic Programming Language Model	90
Layered Architecture of Programming Languages	91
Implementation: Compiled vs Interpreted vs Hybrid	91
What Difference Does It Make?	91
Portability	92
Performance	92
Maintainability	93
Reliability	93
Features	93
Conclusion	94

Chapter 14 - *Software Releases, Updates & Upgrades* 95
Software Development 95
  Scale 96
  Fast or Safe 98
  Agile, Lean, Fast & Safe? 98
  Look & Feel 99
Why So Many New Versions? 99
Releases 99
Updates 100
Upgrades 100
  Stability (Instability) 101

Chapter 15 - *The Perfect Bug Report* 102
  The Help Desk 102
The Perfect Bug Report 102
  The Five W's 102
Bad Bug Reports 103
  The Wrong Foot 103
  Asymmetrical Relationship 104
  Vague & Negative 104
Debugging: The End Goal 104
Classify the Issue 105
  A Bug 105
  User Confusion 106
  Enhancement In Disguise 106
A Repeatable Case 107
Forensic Investigation 107

Part VI - *HTML, SQL & XML*   108

Chapter 16 - *HTML Overview*   109
Hyper-Text   109
Markup Language   109
The World Wide Web   110
  URLs   110
  Web Client/Server   111
  Web Page Layered Architecture   112
HTML Example   112
  Sample HTML Document   112
  Rendered Version   113
Real Life Complexities   113
  Common Gateway Interface (CGI)   114
  Cascading Style Sheets (CSS)   114
  Browser Scripting   115
  Java Applets   116
  The Net Effect   116

Chapter 17 - *Structured Query Language (SQL)*   118
Who Created SQL?   118
Application Program Interface (API)   118
  Common Functions   118
  Privileged Functions   118
Report Generation   119
SQL As API & UI   119
SQL Statements   120

SQL Select Statement ... 120

Chapter 18 - *Extensible Markup Language (XML)* ... 123
What Is XML? ... 123
   Electronic Data Interchange (EDI) ... 123
   Data Models ... 123
   Optional History Lesson ... 124
   XML Encodes Data Models ... 125
   XML Encodes Meta-Data ... 126
XML Is Here To Stay ... 126

Part VII - *Conclusion* ... 127

Chapter 19 - *Conclusion* ... 128
Man Behind the Curtain ... 128
Help IT Help You ... 128
Reasonable Expectations ... 128
Culture Clash ... 128
Empathy & Expertise ... 129
Final Word ... 129

Index ... 130

Preface

Totally Rewritten

Way back when in 2008, I wrote a book intended to answer questions I was constantly asked as part of my consulting practice in IT. That book was the first edition of this book.

Sadly, that edition of this book was out-of-date almost as soon as it was published. (And, as many of my friends and colleagues were very happy to point out, getting more out-of-date every day.) Like so many other part-time authors writing about rapidly-changing topics, I made a mental note to update the book as soon as I could get to it.

Time passed. Lots of time. I left a copy of the first edition on my desk and it became festooned with notes about what was no longer relevant. More time passed.

Seven years later, that opportunity finally presented itself. But seven years is a very long time in the computer hardware and software game, so I felt that an update would not be enough.

So I gritted my teeth and rewrote the book from scratch: a new outline and entirely rewritten text. I did not use the original text. I did not even re-read the original text.

If nothing else, I can say that this edition is more up-to-date.

February 2018

Part I

Background

This part is intended to provide context for the rest of the book.

The first chapter describes who would benefit from this book and what workplace interactions might be improved by reading this book.

The second chapter discusses abstraction in general and how we use abstraction in Information Technology (IT) specifically.

The third chapter gives a glimpse of how the other half lives, and tries to give the reader a sense of how Tech Support's days can go wrong.

About This Book

This book is structured as a handbook. To me, a handbook [1] is intended to be used in two ways: first, read it through to get a grounding in this topic and second, consult it piecemeal as needed.

In order to support skipping around the book, the chapters are deliberately short and targeted. In theory you could start with either the Table of Contents to find a page number for a topic and start reading. Or you could start with Index to find a page number for a specific term and start reading.

What Do We Mean By 'IT'?

If you work in an office, you already have some idea of what IT is. If you were born after 1980, you have used lots of IT without really thinking about it. If you were born before 1980, you have watched IT go from simple office automation to so much more:

- The default way we communicate

- The way we create documents

- The way we print those documents

- The way we scan those documents

- The way we store and retrieve information

But the goal of this book is for you to have more than some idea of what some of IT does: instead, the goal is for you to have a basic understanding of what all of it does.

A basic understanding of IT is not a modest goal. At this point, IT is so complex and varied that very few people really understand most of it and very people indeed understand it completely. Which may explain why excellence in technical support can be hard to come by.

IT Organizations

In my experience, IT organizations come in three sizes: small, medium and large. The mission is the same in all three sizes, but the experience of working in them, and the kind of technology generally found in them, tends to differ in predictable ways. Whenever I feel that it is relevant, I will distinguish between the small IT, medium IT and large IT. We will return to the differences between different sized organizations in a later chapter.

Why Read This Book?

The executive summary is this: read this book to help you have better and more effective interactions with Information Technology (IT) and more productive interactions with Tech Support in the workplace.

The long version is this:

- If you are an IT outsider but you find that you need to deal with IT folks in order to do your job, then you may want to read this book.

- If you find IT folks to be different to the point of being a foreign culture, then you may want to read this book.

- If you find explanations of IT matters boring to the point of hallucination, then you may want to read this book.

- If you are tired of not understanding the technology you work with everyday, then you may want to read this book.

- If you are frustrated by how often IT seems flaky or mysterious in its failure modes and by how often its keepers seem incapable of explaining what is going on, then you may want to read this book.

Why Write This Book?

It might be helpful to know who I am and where I am coming from; if not, then feel free to skip this section. In fact, this book is structured with skipping around in mind.

I must confess that I have an ulterior motive for writing this book: I am hoping that a basic understanding of IT will lubricate interactions with Tech Support. Because many of the questions I am asked about IT are actually questions about how to talk to Tech Support.

The most common complaint I hear about Tech Support is that their communications skills are poor (and their manners and their hygiene and their fashion sense, but those are all issues I consider to be outside my area of expertise and therefore not my problem).

This apparent inability to communicate is the most common reason people come to me for input and advice. I find myself being asked over and over again to mediate, to translate, to "talk to our tech people because they listen to you."

This is not a particularly fulfilling way to spend one's time, even if I often am paid to do it. [2] Surely the slight adjustments I make to the user's complaints are not that hard for people to learn to make for themselves? Surely managers who need to ask for service from IT departments can learn to make requests which are more likely to produce the desired outcome?

The desire to test this belief is the primary reason I wrote this book. I hope that by showing how to restate the age-old the question "Why doesn't X work?" or the merely irritating complaint "something somewhere went wrong!" I can help users skip over the frustration of why IT people are not better communicators and explainers and jump right to using IT people for the jobs they were hired to do: maintaining and adapting IT to their particular environment.

CHAPTER 1 — About This Book

My Qualifications

People keep asking me these kinds of questions because of my job and my approach to it. My job is IT designer, creator, implementor, inventor, architect, whatever we are calling ourselves today. My approach is conversational: I happen to be fast enough to do much of this work in real-time, which means I am happy to do it while users or colleagues are sitting beside me so we can have a conversation about what the tech does and why.

Once you get into conversational mode with a large number of people about a small family of technologies, it is hard to get out of that mode. And if you are going to talk to lots of people about specific technology for a large number of hours, people are going to come to view you as their technology guru, or their technology confessor, or their technology therapist.

You become their technology oracle even if you constantly point out helpful facts such as "I did not write this (or any other) version of Windows" or "I did not configure that" or "I would just be guessing."

Upon hearing me complain about yet another such interaction, a friend of mine wearily explained that this was a simple mystery to solve: people keep asking me these questions because I keep giving them an answer. "I don't know" is better than "Go away." "I don't know but" is even better than "I don't know." "I don't know, I guess it would have to be one of these things, you are going to have to be more precise" is not only better, but helpful even because it is part of a dialog. IT people rarely feel that they have the time to enter into a dialog over bug reports and even more rarely enjoy such conversations. I do not love these conversations, but I do not abhor them.

So there you have it: my own damn fault. I enjoy a bit of detective work and I am comfortable with the process of matching up a user's experience with the fundamental properties of IT. I gather that this can make me a tiresome dinner companion but it seems to make me a solid second choice for those times when Tech Support has failed you.

Examples

If a picture is worth a thousand words then an example must be worth at least five hundred. In that spirit, I will try to put a real life example whenever I can.

Let's Break It Down

In order to make the massive mosaic that is IT more digestible, we are going to break IT down into digestible pieces, using a conceptual model called "layered architecture." This abstraction is often used by technology developers to design and build IT in the first place.

When we say "layer" we mean a distinct component of a piece of information technology. By convention we order these distinct layers with the most concrete (least abstract) at the bottom and the least concrete (most abstract) at the top.

Simple IT Model

Moving from bottom to top, this is our first layered architecture:

1. Hardware (physical devices such as laptops)
2. System software (operating systems such Windows)
3. Application software (such as MS-Word)
4. Networking (such as wifi in a coffee shop)

This is perhaps a bit *too* abstract, so let's consider a specific example: finding directions on your smart phone as you drive down the road.

- Your smart phone itself is the hardware.
- The smart phone's system software is likely either iOS from Apple or a version of Android.

- The app might be any of several, but let us assume Google Maps for simplicity's sake.

- The networking is whatever your mobile carrier uses to send data over its mobile phone network.

Although familiarity has bred contempt, when you perform this apparently simple act you are actually setting off a long chain of events:

- running millions of lines of code [3]

- on several different pieces of hardware many miles apart

- over several different kinds of networking.

That choreographed dance between different computers in different places running different software is pretty complicated, but excellent engineering makes it seem seamless and simple. So much has to go right for it to work, but most of the time, work it does.

When the technology fails, we need to know roughly where to look before we dive deep into the details. The layered architecture model gives us control over complexity by allowing us to move easily from the very high level to the low level. Once the overview has identified a layer we wish to understand, we can apply the layered architecture to a layer itself, allowing us to drill down into the details.

Specifically, subsequent chapters will identify layers which will, themselves, be divided into layers in yet more subsequent chapters.

Chapter 1 End Notes

[1] My model for a handbook is the various lab handbooks I used in the dim, dark days of highschool. I loved the fact that I could read them from cover to cover, just to get a sense of what was in them, but refer to specific chapters later as needed.

[2] I cannot escape the memory of one of the Oz books in which a character is employed as an English-to-English translator between the North of the Kingdom and the South of the Kingdom. Amusing unless you have to live it.

[3] http://www.informationisbeautiful.net/visualizations/million-lines-of-code/

Abstraction & IT

IT has a very strange property: it combines large amounts of abstraction with large amounts of concrete nuts-and-bolts electrical engineering.

Sadly, abstraction is always imperfect: the nuts-and-bolts have a way of poking through the veil, through the clean, simple lines that abstraction can provide. As we will see below, this imperfection is more likely to cause friction between users and Tech Support than to make my explanations faulty.

What 'Abstraction' Means Here

Abstraction is a broad topic but in this context we mean high-level, general and broad descriptions of technology at the functional level.

By "functional level" I mean ignoring details and considering pieces of technology only in terms of most basic function. For example, the typical PC keyboard produces scan codes which allow the PC [1] to distinguish both which key is pressed (the left shift versus the right shift) and how long the key is pressed. But if everything is working properly, we can think of a keyboard as just producing printable characters just as a typewriter used to do. When something goes wrong, this abstraction may have to be cast aside as we look for the fault.

Abstraction Pros

There are many ways in which abstraction is powerful and useful:

- Abstraction is great at controlling complexity.

- It is a powerful shorthand when detail is not needed.

- It is a way for people to give and receive explanations without requiring a deep knowledge of the topic at hand.

- It is often the best way to see the forest for the trees.

Abstraction Cons

The downsides of abstraction all stem from the fact that abstractions are all, to some degree, false. Simplification can become oversimplification if the circumstances change.

On Balance

Despite its potential drawbacks, we will be relying heavily on abstraction to explain IT concepts in this book. But while we are reliant on abstraction, we are not blind to its faults.

As I said at the beginning of this chapter, abstraction hides complexity so well that when the inevitable failure occurs, the innocent user is often unpleasantly surprised by the failure and completely at a loss about what to do about the failure.

The unpleasant surprise and feelings of helplessness that the failures of abstraction can cause are all too often the cause of friction and ill will between users and Tech Support. But this kind of failure is unlikely to be such a problem in this book. I will endeavor to point out likely failures of the abstractions we use as we go along.

Example: The Cloud

A computing abstraction which is nearly ubiquitous at the moment is "The Cloud." Since the networking technology that runs the Internet [2] is non-directional, IT people were in the habit of representing the Internet as a cloud, which they tended to call "the ether." When computing services started being delivered on servers over the Internet, the diagrams showed the services coming out of a cloud and some marketing person said "the services are in the Cloud!" and all attempts to correct them failed. The abstraction was so appealing that it was pointless to point out that the "cloud" is merely the delivery mechanism for servers and not a source of service.

CHAPTER 2 *Abstraction & IT* 23

So enjoy the abstraction of a cloud into which requests are put and from which responses are drawn, unless and until something goes wrong.

Levels of Abstraction

Unlike Philosophy, in IT we have levels of abstraction. For example, source code is somewhat abstract. The executable produced from the source code is rather less abstract. The executable, loaded and running on a particular computer, is pretty concrete.

Entering your name and email address into an email client is somewhat abstract but emails with your name and email address are rather less abstract.

Layered Architecture

We will be making use of the levels of abstraction throughout the book in form of the "layered architecture" concept which we will put to use in the very next section.

LAYERS OF THE CLOUD

Here is a simplified layered architecture for the Cloud, using pulling up a web page from a server as our example:

1. A client computer runs a browser which allows the user to follow a link to get a web page.

2. A message is sent over a network which connects the client to the server specified in the link.

3. A server computer which accepts the request, finds the requested web page and then sends the web page back to the client.

Chapter 2 End Notes

[1] Actually, the keyboard driver, which is part of the PC's system software, does this job but "PC" is a convenient abstraction.

[2] The networking technology that runs the Internet is the Internet Protocol (IP), which we will examine in detail in the chapter on networking.

Sympathy For Tech Support

Since much of this book describes unsatisfactory interactions with Tech Support, one might be forgiven for assuming that I have a problem with Tech Support. However, I do not. They have a tough job. Sometimes I am Tech Support. I have spent plenty of time on both sides of this divide. I have been the Tech guy beyond frustrated by end users. I have been the end user utterly furious at the dismissive imperiousness of Tech Support.

Not that all interactions with Tech Support are unsatisfactory, just too many of them.

Tech Support is not a generally warmly regarded segment of the workforce. I would say that they have surpassed lawyers as being the butt of work-related jokes. Dilbert is their avatar, even though Dilbert is mostly about how technologists get it from all sides. [1]

Culture Clash

Tech Support often chastises users for not being able to explain themselves clearly. Users often grind their teeth at having to know "magic words" in order to get help. Equipping you with effective vocabulary is certainly a goal of this book.

There is more to having a satisfactory Tech Support experience than vocabulary, although vocabulary is important. In addition to understanding a few basic concepts and using a few simple, clear formats to report issues, there is also the question of culture.

Tech Support is generally about making sure things work the way that they are supposed to. Note that I wrote "making sure **things** work the way that they are supposed to" and not "supporting your colleagues in their jobs by using technology." It would be great if the second statement were true, but it is not: Tech Support is often judged by some poorly-chosen metrics: time on the phone, number of tickets closed, etc. These metrics are not about user satisfaction, or user productivity, or Tech Support politeness. And Tech Support staff figure this out pretty quickly.

This cultural clash is compounded by the fact that, traditionally, the typical Tech Support person is not a people person. I hope that this will change as society changes and as tech becomes less of a religion and more commonplace.

But for now, in my experience, the face of Tech Support is youngish, maleish, whiteish and socially awkward. This profile worked well for tech maintenance people in the field in the days of yore. [2] Alas the days of yore are gone forever and this profile is not a terrific fit with today's office environment.

However it came to be, Tech Support culture is generally engineering-like and generally about the facts and demonstrable success or failure. This is the root of a common complaint with Tech Support: they do not see what is wrong with saying "You may not like it, but this is the way this technology is supposed to work." Or worse, "There is nothing to fix, it isn't broken. Yes I can see that you cannot do your job with things as they are." Or worst of all, "You should change how you do your job to fit the technology because this is how the technology works."

Anatomy of Mutually Unsatisfying Tech Support

The archetypal bad interaction between users and Tech Support goes like this:

1. A critical failure occurs. Tech Support is called in.

2. The users are already angry, which makes Tech Support defensive.

3. Tech Support finds out that the bug report is trivially but crucially misworded, making the Tech Support plan useless. Tech Support is not very polite in pointing this out. Users find the distinction trivial and feel that Tech Support is trying to weasel out of responsibility;

4. Tech Support finds out that a critical assumption they made is wrong, which is equal parts embarrassing and infuriating. Users acknowledge that there has been a crescendo of issues over many weeks but the users heroically soldiered on through the issues until their patience was exhausted. Now the users are fed up and Tech Support is furious that they

missed the chance to nip this issue in the bud.

5. Tech Support resolves the issue and leaves with their sense that users are evil, rude dullards re-enforced. Users go home with another story of surly incompetence and finger-pointing to tell their uninterested spouses.

This does not have to happen. If you have a sense of how things are supposed to work, you can learn to give gentle warnings of issues. If you have a sense of how the technology is set up, you can explore optimizing it for your workflow in a more relaxed and productive manner. Because everyone is right and everyone is wrong: users are (unintentionally) cheerfully obstructive; Tech Support is (unintentionally) opaque and inconsiderate. But users are also just trying to get their jobs done and so is Tech Support. Everyone involved would love to have less drama in their lives and more stability. And we can get there.

Reasons To Pity Tech Support

It is small consolation if someone has just ruined your day, but there is a good chance that your local Tech Support person is having a worse day than you are. Far from being a golden age of IT, the early 21st century is in turning into a nightmare for many IT departments. The two pillars of this temple of dysfunction are Complexity and Compartmentalization.

Complexity

The current IT landscape is bewilderingly complex and frighteningly heterogenous. There are so many devices and so many overlapping areas of functionality: the fax machine is a printer, and a print server, and a file server, and a scan-to-email device. So many functions, all advertised to any and all PCs! So much to support or turn off or try to turn off. Even if you buy all your core technology from a single vendor, you are likely to discover that your single vendor bought some of it from other vendors and that not all the devices work the same way. Or even work together. Or worse, they do work together but if you take the defaults then you make things crazy complicated.

I was once baffled by the problems users had sharing files between two very similar servers. With a painful amount of detective work, I found out that one of the servers was running a virtual server (don't ask) which pretended to be a PC sharing files to another PC, but the other "PC" was another similar server pretending to be a PC because all the servers were configured to pretend to be PCs because that is what is mostly in offices, right? It was amazing that this arrangement worked at all, but it did not work well. Even though the entire set up cost more than you want to know. But the answer to the question "why does this suck?" was not easy to answer and was impossible to fix.

In large organizations, the reason to pity Tech Support is this complexity: they have been tasked with managing a giant portfolio of very different technologies. Worse, previous generations of technology are running and need to be kept running even as the infrastructure mutates and morphs over time. They are just trying to hold their position against the tide. They do not need you telling them that the printer is jammed again.

Small organizations have less technology, but often still more than they can handle. Users demand it. Vendors promise that it will just work. Most of the time it does just work (once you go through the painful set up). But when it does fail, there is just so much to debug.

Compartmentalization

With the rise of complexity has come the increasing bureaucracy of Tech Support. In the beginning there was the mainframe and the people who ran jobs on it, and hung tapes, and made sure the air conditioner was working, etc.

Then came the explosion of apps, which meant splitting out the Help Desk so that people who were nicer than the backroom guys but less knowledgeable could take your call.

Once PCs hit the scene, the Help Desk was joined by Desktop Support. But PCs forced a revolution in networking, so we needed a Network Group since so many desktop issues and app issues were network issues in disguise.

PCs meant word processing which added a giant printing headache: no longer a central resource, desktop publishing meant desktop printing for the lucky few and shared (departmental) printing for the rest of us. Printing was also often heavily dependant on networking, but somewhat on the apps which submitted the print jobs and a bit on Desktop Support for the PCs which ran the apps.

PCs meant reporting tools which promised that end users could make their own reports. That promise of end user independence resulted in end users asking endless questions about database structure and data elements and so we needed Database Guys.

Database Guys were not enough because reporting tools are often resource hogs on their host PCs so many of the issues are actually Desktop Support, so we needed Desktop Support guys. Worse, reports are still frequently printed so some of the issues are actually printing issues and the data is all remote so some of the issues are actually networking issues. So we needed Printing Guys and Network Guys and that got pretty complex pretty quickly.

In large organizations, debugging across lines of responsibility can be difficult because as a Tech Support person you might not have access to the network configuration, or the passwords for the server, or something else that you need. In a poorly run large organization, you have to be senior management to get all the kinds of attention you need from all the different groups in order to make sure that your IT all works as expected.

In small organizations, outsourcing often means that you just do not know who to call, or what to do if the company who runs your network says it is your ISP, but the ISP says that it is your network.

Sometimes There Is No Answer

Thanks to complexity and compartmentalization sometimes there is no answer. At least no answer that is accessible. Consider the following real-life example:

An Example from Real Life

The example will use terms and concepts we have yet to cover but will give you something to review once we do cover these concepts.

Video Call Failure

My wife works in a small organization. There is not much in the way of in-house Tech Support, so she relies on vendors for support. Sometimes that simply does not work because the problem is in the interaction of different pieces of technology.

In this particular case, she was trying to debug the sudden failure of a teleconferencing app with the following architecture:

1. An iPad client which provides the user interface

2. A Mac Mini server which provides the actual video call

3. The client and server communicate over a wireless network

4. The server connects to other servers over the public Internet

The problem seemed to be between the client and server because the server could be used to make video calls on its own.

Since the client and server are on the same wireless network, she went to the local Tech Support folks to ask them if anything had changed. Nothing had changed locally. The wireless network was working for other purposes. So no joy there.

Perhaps the issue was with the client or the server hardware, so she rebooted them, separately, then together. Repeatedly. No change.

Perhaps the issue was with the vendor's software. They were skeptical, but they asked for a network trace. My wife did not know how to do that, so she asked me and it seemed to be imprudent to refuse.

I ran through the local networking and it seemed fine. I confirmed that the client and server were both accessible on the local network from a third machine and were both visible to each other.

I have a laptop for debugging network activities because part of my job is to debug distributed information systems. So I know what a network trace is and how to make one. But in this case, the trace was not very interesting: it showed that the client went looking for the server and the server did not answer. The trace showed a lack of response. But a trace that lacks something is not interesting. Or useful.

I googled the software base to find out which port this company's software uses to communicate over the network. I found out the port, so I dusted off more of my distributed system debugging tool kit and prodded the server on the specified port by hand, just as the client was doing. No response. I used another tool to try to connect to the server. No response. I used a tool to connect and listen to the server in case it was broadcasting some kind of error message. Nothing. I started to pack up to regretfully inform my wife that I had done all I could but to no avail. I had my notes and was going to dump all this on the vendor and try to browbeat them into doing *something*.

Before I could make a bug report to the vendor, my wife hailed me. "It works! What did you do?" she said. "I did many, many things and nothing worked," I replied. "Well, it works now!" she said.

For the next several days I kept checking and the mysterious failure did not reappear before I got tired of asking and they got tired of answering.

So where does that leave us? Aside from the vague sense of unease with which I am left, and the strong sense that IT can be deeply flaky with which my wife is left, here are the take-aways from this example to which we will return in this book:

NOTHING TO DO

There was nothing for any of the apparently unhelpful Tech Support to do: the entire complicated set up was working one day, then it wasn't; now it works again and so one could argue that there was nothing for Tech Support to do.

SO COMPLICATED

The apparently simple set up is actually very complicated, with lots of moving parts: a client, a server, a wireless network, a connection to the Internet.

SO COMPARTMENTALIZED

This apparently simple act of making a video call crosses many boundaries between different vendors so there is ample opportunity for finger-pointing and blame-shifting. This is an unwanted side effect of having lots of technology from lots of different vendors: Tech Support becomes compartmentalized with no one being actually responsible for solving your particular problem.

SMALL COMPANY, LARGE SUPPORT BURDEN

This is the tragedy of the small organization's Tech Support: there is a large amount of technology even in a small organization.

Understanding For Tech Support

The next time you are frustrated by Tech Support's seeming indifference or lack of action, spare a moment to consider that they might just be stuck. They might be overwhelmed by the complexity or stymied by the compartmentalization.

Then take a deep breath and restate your issue using what you are going to learn in the rest of this book.

(Sometimes Just A Jerk)

Here is a story I try to keep in mind when I want to quell the urge to judge my colleagues: the wife of a colleague works as psychiatrist. She used to warn against overanalyzing people for laypeople and professionals alike. When it was time to discuss an unpleasant patient, she dismissed the various diagnoses of personality disorder that were bandied about. "Sometimes the patient is just a jerk," she said. So while I urge sympathy and empathy for Tech Support in general, I recognize that sometimes the simple truth is that whoever you are dealing with might just be a jerk.

Chapter 3 End Notes

[1] After hearing so many complaints about Tech Support, I started an informal survey of my friends about their workplaces. One out of about a dozen said that she likes their "tech guy." Those are some long odds of finding mutually satisfactory IT relationships.

[2] When I started in Tech, most of my workdays were spent in dimly lit, windowless server rooms.

Part II

Hardware: Getting Concrete

This part is intended to give the reader a basic background in the hardware that runs IT.

Chapter four applies the methodology we introduced in Part I to the traditional computer.

Chapter five applies this same methodology to the nontraditional computers that begin to proliferate in our lives.

Chapter six gives an unavoidably long but shallow description of computer networking which we will need to help us in later chapters.

Traditional Computers

Let us consider the traditional computer, first in its abstract form and then in its three most common configurations: the desktop, the server and the laptop. At their core, all of these variants are essentially the same with some minor differences in "form factor."

The Basic Overview from Chapter 1

We will be using the model we introduced in the previous chapter, with a very slight upgrade:

1. Hardware

2. Peripherals (devices such as scanners or digital cameras)

3. System software

4. Application software

Layers of Hardware

In the classic computing device, there are layers within the hardware layer:

- A processor to execute the instructions which make up software; usually called the Central Processing Unit (CPU).

- Random Access Memory, to hold the instructions to be executed; usually called RAM.

- Input hardware to gather input to put into the device, such as a keyboard or a touch screen; the input half of the User Interface (UI).

- Display hardware to allow output to be viewed by the user; the output half of the UI. [1]

- Persistent storage which allows the computer to store data across sessions and which is like RAM, but slower and "non-volatile" [2] . The most common technology for persistent storage is the spinning magnetic disk, usually called "a hard disk." But recently the kind of solid state technology found in USB thumb drives has become more and more common for this job, especially in laptops.

Peripherals

Peripheral devices are pieces of hardware which are not tightly physically integrated with the rest of the hardware. The peripherals are usually not required in order to use the computer; instead, they are plugged into special slots or connected with cables or connected over short-range radio links such as Bluetooth.

The Typical Traditional Computer

Thus the typical traditional computing device: a "system unit" which holds the CPU, the RAM and the disk; a keyboard for input; a monitor for output and perhaps a directly-connected printer as a peripheral.

The Glories of System Software

Software comes in parcels called "programs." Programs are stored in files and the files are stored on disk. This is a bit of an oversimplification but for now we will just think of a programs as a chunk of runnable stuff which do a particular job.

Software comes in two varieties: system software and application software ("apps" for short). In the usual case, the system software is the Operating System (OS) which can also be broken down into layers as we will see below.

Most of the time, all we want from the OS is to launch apps and support apps while they run.

System programs are different from application programs in that their focus is limited functionality with no faults and the greatest speed that certainty can allow. If the OS is stable, the device has a chance of being useful; being fast is only interesting in useful devices.

So who launches the OS? The process of launching the OS is called "booting" which is short for "boot strapping" from the old adage about pulling oneself up by one's bootstraps.

Booting the device is the process of launching the OS so that it can launch apps and support them while they run.

While launching and running apps is a large part of what the OS does, the OS is also a referee of sorts: it adjudicates requests for access to resources and it referees between apps, putting the apps to sleep when it is not their turn to run and waking them up when it is their turn to run.

The strict requirements on the OS tend to keep the designs as simple as possible and the implementations also as simple as possible. The OS can be thought of as having only two layers: the kernel (the core) and the drivers (system software which provides the kernel with a way to interact with peripherals).

Application Software

Apps are generally what users see and use when they interact with a computer. Smart phones have made explaining apps much easier: they are self-contained bits of software providing a particular broad function, such as driving or walking directions (Google Maps), or spreadsheet management (Microsoft Excel), or playing music (Apple's iTunes).

As for launching and running apps, the kernel does all that: finding the app on disk, copying its instructions from the disk into RAM, then executing those instructions when the app's turn arrives.

As for access to RAM and peripherals and the disk (through drivers), the kernel sets limits and enforces policy and the apps must humbly obey.

Apps are the reason normal people have computers in the first place. Apps are the source of most of the pain and agony of tech support. When computers fail, apps are usually the culprit. This is the apps conundrum: they are supposed to do whatever users might want, but unbridled flexibility for users often leads to unstable computers.

In other words, in order to develop fast and functional apps, the OS sometimes has to allow more than is prudent; however an OS which does not allow cool apps does not gain any marketshare.

Early versions of Microsoft Windows blurred the distinction between driver and kernel and between app and OS. The result was an Office suite which was commendably feature-filled on a platform which was lamentably unstable and prone to crashing. Users evidently preferred features to stability, as during this time Microsoft was reputed to be the greatest engine of wealth creation in American history.

Getting Specific

Now that we have an overview of the classical computer, let us consider the most common variants of that classical architecture: the server, the desktop and the laptop.

So What Makes A Server?

There is some confusion about the term "server" because IT is so changing and so flexible that today's clear lines are tomorrow's blurry tangle. A detailed discussion of software server versus hardware server would be premature but a quick explanation is required to make this section intelligible.

SERVER OR SERVER?

In the good old days, I could say "mainframe" when I wanted to talk about the archetypal "big computer," housed in the basement or backroom or some other dark, overly air-conditioned place in which I have spent so many well-paid but unpleasant hours. But fashion has made "mainframe" obsolete and thanks to the rise of the Client/Server app architecture, sometimes "server" means "app software which answers a certain kind of question" and sometimes "server" means "a computer not intended for direct use by humans but rather to host a software server."

SERVER FORM FACTOR

A hardware server is fundamentally similar to the classic computer in architecture with a few notable exceptions:

- I/O (Input/Output) is generally simpler and has higher capacity than a user machine. For example, servers often have more processing power and faster, higher throughput network connections than desktops or laptops.

- Storage (disk) is generally faster in performance and generally greater in size than desktops or laptops.

- Display is generally mediocre and often shared between servers, because system administrators generally only need to interact with one hardware server at a time.

For small IT, the hardware server is generally a computer rather like a desktop.

For medium IT or large IT, the hardware server is often in a server farm. A common arrangement for a server farm is the "pizza box" in a rack in a machine room.

So What Makes A Desktop?

A desktop's "form factor" (physical form) is generally one of these:

- A "tower" which is a system unit that is vertical and on its edge. Usually the tower (which is sometimes used for servers for small IT) is to the side with the monitor next to it and the keyboard in front of the monitor.

- A common desktop which is a system unit that is horizontal and on its long side. Usually the system unit is used as a base for the monitor and the keyboard is in front of the monitor.

- An uncommon arrangement is a rather fat monitor with the system unit behind the monitor and the keyboard underneath the monitor/system unit.

So What Makes A Laptop?

A laptop is defined by having a clam shell form factor with the monitor on the upper shell and a system unit in the lower shell with a built-in keyboard on top of the system unit, as well as a built-in battery.

Chapter 4 End Notes

[1] Most displays are technically peripherals, but since they are often required by the user to make the computer usable, displays are often not thought of as peripheral.

[2] In this context, "non-volatile" means that the RAM keeps its values even if the power is shut off.

Nontraditional Computing Devices

Why is there a chapter on nontraditional computer devices in a book on IT for managers? There are two reasons: first, thanks to Bring Your Own Device (BYOD) policies, nontraditional computing devices abound in many workplaces and workplace IT has to support them.

Second, nontraditional computer devices illustrate an issue which is at the heart of many unsatisfying encounters with IT: the holes in abstractions are deep and dangerous. They are a fine illustration of the problems IT has with abstraction which we have already covered in a previous chapter.

Sample Nontraditional Computers

The nontraditional forms of classical computing devices are many and varied. A representative sample of this wide class of computer devices is given below, but since we have business bent in this book, only a couple will be featured in this chapter:

- The smart phone

- The tablet (touch screen or stylus)

- The Digital Video Recorder (DVR)

- The cable set top box

- Recent model year cars

- Digital cameras

- Digital scanners with built-in networking

- Printers with built-in print servers

The Smart Phone

The smart phone is a pocket computer with two kinds of wireless networking and an icon interface. The smart phone offers just about all the services that a traditional workplace desktop offers: email, messaging, web browsing, even limited document handling and spreadsheet viewing.

The smart phone generally is so well behaved that users often forget that the smart phone is a computer. A computer that needs a network connection to perform many of these functions just like any other computer. Smart phones run apps, they download data from other computers and upload data to other computers.

But when an app goes berserk, the abstraction has a hole in it: the OS does not provide any way for a user to monitor the functioning of apps: we can kill apps, we can delete them, we can reboot our phones or our tablets, but we cannot do much more than that to correct their behavior.

We also have very few options when it comes to monitoring what apps are doing and why. Alas, the list of reasons to worry about smart phone apps is not short:

- Smart phones are digital cameras whose images can be part of what is uploaded.

- Smart phones are telephones with microphones whose digital recordings can be part of what is uploaded.

- Smart phones are GPS handsets whose location data points can be part of what is uploaded. Smart phones connect to cell phone towers in addition to wireless access points.

- Smart phones are blue tooth servers which can silently and automatically connect to various nearby devices which can either be a boon (wireless earbuds) or a bane (evil devices invading your privacy).

The next time the IT department at work grumbles about the effort of supporting smart phones, remember this long list of functions and all the implied liabilities and risks. Convenient, yes; secure, generally not.

Tablets

Tablets, such as iPads or Android tablets or Amazon tablets or the Windows Surface tablets, are between desktops and smart phones: sort of a smart phone with a bigger screen, but not quite.

Like the smart phone, the tablet is a mobile computer, often with two kinds of wireless networking and usually an icon interface. The tablet is, in many ways, a giant smart phone. It, too, offers just about all the services that a traditional workplace desktop offers: email, messaging, web browsing, even limited document handling and spreadsheet viewing.

Since the tablet has a laptop-ish feel and is often used in a laptop-ish way, users usually are quite aware that their tablet is a computer. Tablets use a network connection to perform many of these functions and run apps; they also download data from other computers and then upload data to other computers.

Tablets and smart phones are also alike in that when an app goes berserk, the abstraction has a hole in it: the OS does not provide any way for a user to monitor the functioning of apps: we can kill apps, we can delete them, we can reboot our phones, but we cannot do much more than that.

And like the smart phone, the list of reasons to worry about tablet apps is not short:

- They often are digital cameras whose images can be part of what is uploaded.

- To support teleconferencing, tablets also are equipped with microphones whose digital recordings can be part of what is uploaded.

- Some tablets also are GPS-enabled and so also have location data points which can be part of what is uploaded. Often we think of tablets as LAN-only devices, but many tablets have the necessary hardware to use mobile phone networks (i.e. connect to cell phone towers) and so can leak information even when those tablets are out of the office or out of the home.

The IT department probably also grumbles about tablets as well as smart phones and also with good reason.

Networked Printers

Once upon a time, a computer printer was connected directly to the one and only mainframe which had a printer connected directly to it. [1]

Then came the Client/Server era. A computer printer was connected directly to a server computer which accepted requests over the network and printed whatever the requests asked it to print. Any computer on the network could use the printing protocol to make requests.

Soon after we had printers with network cables. These were "networked" printers which meant that the printer had a little computer inside it running the printing protocol. The abstract is simple: you plug the "printer" into the network and voila! a printer server appears on your network, and your desktops and other computers can print over the network.

This abstraction, while enticing (who wants to set up and maintain a print server?) has its limits. When something goes wrong with a computer which is acting as a print server, you have all the usual resources for debugging: a keyboard, a monitor, process monitoring tools, etc. When something goes wrong with a "networked printer" you have nothing. The concept of printer does not have much of a user interface. About all it offers is the ability to power cycle it, which is a fancy way of saying "turning it off and then back on."

BYOD To Work

If you bring it to work, your nontraditional computing device becomes part of the work network and while your device is great for you, it is a support burden and potential security risk for them. So enjoy your nontraditional computer device responsibly.

CHAPTER 5   *Nontraditional Computing Devices*   45

Marketing & Packaging

There is an entire class of nontraditional computers which are very confusing, thanks to marketing and packaging.

Consider the device made ubiquitous by cable companies, the so-called "cable modem". [2] It often is actually several things:

1. A cable modem to send and receive data from the cable system.

2. A web server to provide a User Interface (UI) to allow more advanced users to configure the device.

3. A DHCP [3] server to provide addresses for the LAN; the DHCP server is controlled via the web UI.

4. A LAN [4] switch or hub to allow the homeowner to make a LAN so the homeowner can connect various computers together.

5. A wireless access point (WAP) for a WLAN [5] so the homeowner can have wireless devices join the LAN.

6. A router to provide access to the WAN [6] so the home owner can search the web.

This would be rather a mouthful, so someone decided to call these "cable modems" for short. Which is a very useful abstraction unless and until it isn't. This abstraction also means that homeowners do not need to know what a WAP is, or a LAN, or a WLAN, or a router, or a DHCP server or any of the rest of it. So why does the "cable modem" have to be somewhere that allows it to broadcast the wireless signal? Mine went in the utility room behind the water heater which did not work well. Luckily I knew why things were not working well.

Repeater

Sometimes you need a device to make your WLAN reach father. That is called a Repeater.

Extender

Sometimes you want to extend wireless networking to other places and you don't mind if you create many small, linked WLANs. That is called an Extender.

Wireless Access Point (WAP)

Sometimes you want to add a WLAN to your LAN. To do that, you need a WAP unless there is already a WAP built into some other device on your network.

Protocol Analyzer

A computer uses a Network Interface Card (NIC) to get data off of a network. The NIC copies data off of the network and onto its host computer. In the usual case, the NIC screens the network traffic and only copies data which is specifically meant for its host computer and ignores any other data.

Sometimes you need to debug a network-based protocol, which means seeing *all* the network traffic, not just the traffic meant for a particular computer.

To see *all* the network traffic, you need not only a computing device with a NIC but also a driver for that NIC which does not follow the rule of only processing packets addressed to that NIC. This allows the Protocol Analyzer to process, store and display *all* network traffic.

The most common use of a Protocol Analyzer is to create a network trace, which is a record of the network activity during a specific time period. That trace, in turn, is used to debug interactions between computers as we will see in a forthcoming example.

Chapter 5 End Notes

[1] In those less enlightened times, we called them "slave printers."

[2] "Modem" is a contraction of MODulator/DEModulator; modems used to be devices which turn data into binary values to be trans-

mitted or received on a phone line or a serial cable. Nowadays "modem" seems to mean "box that sends and receives data across a wire of some sort."

[3] DHCP stands for Dynamic Host Control Protocol and it provides a way to allow a computer to configure itself to use a LAN.

[4] LAN stands for Local Area Network. We will get into this in more detail in a later chapter

[5] WLAN stands for Wireless Local Area Network. This will also be covered in a later chapter.

[6] WAN stands for Wide Area Network which is how LANs are connected to each other. Probably actually a Network Address Translator (NAT) to provide some rudimentary firewall protection and a way for the homeowner who has a private network.

Networking

Computer-to-Computer Networking: everyone sort of knows what it is but very few people actually know how it works. Everyone notices when it does not work, though, because it has become a nearly-essential part of using IT.

(From here on out we will just call it "networking" because "computer-to-computer networking" is too long.)

Layered Architecture of Networks

This is the bare minimum you need to connect two computers together into a physical network:

1. Transport layer: it actually carries data from one place to another.

2. Network interface: it physically connects your computer device to the transport layer.

3. Network protocol: it allows the sending and receiving computers to make sense of the data they receive through the network interface.

Some More Detail

This is a bit more detail for those who like that sort of thing:

Transport Layer

Something has to actually physically transport the data from one place to another, even if that physical transportation is via invisible radio waves moving through the air. Doubt not their physicality, lest you find yourself puzzled by their inability to penetrate many solid objects.

Typically, the transport layer uses either copper wire cables or "wireless" (radio signals moving through the air), or both. Since networks can have many segments, some of them can be wireless while others are wired. I prefer "wired" versus "wireless" but many people use "wifi" instead of "wireless."

Most transport layers are message-oriented which means that they gather data up into chunks and send the chunks along as a unit. If you ever see a parameter called "Maximum Transfer Unit" or "MTU" on a configuration screen somewhere, this is the size of that chunk. Do not change the MTU unless you *really* know what you are doing.

Network Interface

The network interface is usually called a "NIC" (Network Interface Card) in the PC context, or "wireless NIC" if the network is wireless.

The NIC has to match the transport layer, obviously. If you have a wireless network, then you need a wireless NIC to interface to it. If you have a wired network, you need a NIC (and a cable) to interface to it.

Each NIC has a unique identifer called "a MAC address." This ID is supposed to be unique in all the world, so that even if all the world's network-capable devices were simultaneously connected and powered up, no two nodes would have the same transport layer address.

Network Protocol: IP

Once we started connecting computers together, we started needing a common language in which to exchange data and a common set of rules to govern the conversation. Much as social protocol specifies how a polite person behaves at a formal event, so a network protocol specifies how a good citizen computer behaves as a network node.

It has been a long time since I have seen any networking protocol in use other than the Internet Protocol (IP) so I will assume that all networks are IP networks.

As we will see below, IP was created to make the Internet possible. But it is also useful for allowing your PC printer on a shared printer and for supporting your smart phone accessing a search engine from your car as you speed down the highway. IP supports all these different situations, each with different transport layers, because IP does not require or exclude any particular transport layer.

IP ADDRESSES

Just as the layer below has the MAC address to uniquely identify each NIC, so IP has the IP address to uniquely identify each computer. IP addresses are made of four "octets" [1] which are commonly written in "dot notation" like this:

```
192.168.1.5
```

- The first octet is 192

- The second octet is 168

- The third octet is 1

- The fourth octet is 5

The first and second octet together form a "network." In this case, 192.168 define the network.

The third octet is the "subnet" within that network. So 192.168.1 is the subnet.

The fourth octet is the node within this subnet, which gives this particular node 192.168.1.5 as its IP address.

Being nodes in the same network is like living in the same town: you can get from one to another but you need to use the roads to do it.

Being nodes in the same subnet is like having houses on the same cul-de-sac. Even if you are not right next to each other, you can get from one house to another without having to drive or having to know the layout of the town.

So 192.168.1.12 can "see" 192.168.1.5 without any kind of route or any kind of networking help. These nodes can "find" each other with the computer equivalent of sticking their heads out a window and shouting. This kind of networking is gloriously simple to set up and delightfully reliable. This is the most basic kind of LAN and if that is all you need, you are in luck: the abstraction is nearly perfect. Just plug it all in and go.

PACKET-BASED

IP is packet-based, which means that the protocol gathers up data into messages which it calls packets. Much as the layer below transfers in chunks, so this layer transmits in packets.

Transferring in packets allows every node on the network to handle the data properly. Every node can tell which packets are for that node, based on IP address.

Packets are also why IP-based LANs work so well. Imagine that the network is a set of tubes connecting all the computers. Imagine that the packets are marbles which flow around the network. Imagine that every node has a unique color: one is black, one is red and one is white. Every node sees every marble, but does not need to examine the marbles in order to function: the black node picks out the black marbles and lets the rest go by. The white node picks out the white marbles and so on. [2]

In reality, there are no tubes and no marbles but the concept is the same: each NIC reads every packet in the transport layer but each NIC knows which packets are directed at it and only passes those packets up the chain to the host computer. So each host only "sees" packets meant for it.

LAN vs WAN vs WLAN

Networks come in two basic types: local and not-local which we call "local" and "wide area."

- Local Area Networks (LANs): at the transport level this means physically connected to the same network segment; at the IP level this means on the same subnet.

- Wide Area Networks (WANs): at the transport level this means a network of networks which allow two physically separate LANs to communicate; at the IP level this means having routing in place to guide packets on the "hops" needed to get from one subnet to the other.

Sometimes it matters that a LAN or LAN segment is wireless, so we needed a way to talk about that, so this scheme was extended slightly:

- Wireless LANs (WLANs): at the transport level WLAN refers to all the authorized devices with wireless NICs in range of a given wireless access point ("wifi hot spot").

Directing Traffic

In theory, it should not matter if your device is on a LAN and you need that device to access another device on another LAN: that kind of "routing" is available from hardware for the transport layer and is built into IP. But in real life this "network topology" matters more often than you might think.

In order to make two LANs into a single LAN, which creates a *single* LAN at IP-level LAN, you need a device called "a bridge" which copies packets across the networks so the two LANs are fused into one LAN and every node on either network has access to all the nodes on both networks.

In order to get packets from one subnet to another subnet, which creates an IP-level WAN, you need a device called "a router" which knows the path from one subnet to another. The path consists of the IP address of a "gateway" which is how packets get off the LAN to the WAN.

There is an additional wrinkle: in order to make network administration easier, the good folks who defined IP set aside some networks as "private" which means that, by convention, routers are not supposed to route packets to the WAN from them. Thus network architects who use private networks for LANs should be reasonably assured that their private data will not go over the Internet. We will return to this topic in much greater detail in the chapter on Security.

Don't worry if this story does not really make sense to you in the abstract: much of networking becomes much clearer in context. And we will use a previous example as context at the end of this chapter.

Assigning IP Addresses

When IP was defined, there were only servers and not many of them. Furthermore, there really were only local (same subnet) servers and remote (over the WAN) servers.

Static IP Addresses

With only a few computers to which to assign IP addresses, and servers to boot, it was easy enough to manually assign what are now called "static IP addresses." Servers tend to run all the time and to be replaced only rarely. Furthermore, even if the hardware is replaced, there is good reason to keep the IP address the same so that all the clients can still avail themselves of whatever service or services the server provides.

Dynamic IP Addresses: DHCP

When the revolution of client computing arrived, suddenly there was a huge increase in the number of addresses needed and these addresses were not needed all the time or even to be consistent over time, since clients need to find servers but servers merely need to respond to clients at whatever IP address the client used. At first, system administrators tried to manually assign IP addresses to all the client computers. This worked poorly for two reasons:

1. Since octets can only represent 0 through 255, there is a theoretical limit of 256 values for a subnet. In practice, 255 is the broadcast address so bad things will happen if you assign 255 to a network node; 0 is only valid in some IP addressing schemes. Therefore, to be safe, any subnet can only have 254 nodes within it. And you get to 254 nodes much faster than you might think.

2. Since client computers tend to be shut off much of the time, and sometimes taken out of service without telling any

sysadmins, sysadmins found that their precious IP addresses were assigned to computers which didn't need them at the moment (shut off) or ever again (decommissioned).

A solution to this problem of client IP addresses was provided by one of the companies most responsible for the proliferation of client machines (desktop PCs): Microsoft. The solution was the Dynamic Host Configuration Protocol (DHCP). DHCP allows a client computer to request an IP address--remember that NICs have a MAC address, so NICs can send and receive data over a network without an IP address. The client requests an IP address from a DHCP server, which gives sys admins a measure of control. Each address assignment comes with a "lease" which expires if not renewed. So when a client computer is put into a closet, or given away, the lease expires and the address is returned to the pool.

This is another abstraction which is terrific unless and until it fails: you turn on a computer device, it configures itself as a client and then it all just works. What if your computer device does not become properly configured? There is very little that a layperson can do to debug that problem.

Worse, these days clients sometimes act as servers to other clients, so if an IP address changes at the whim of the DHCP server, the app which depends on a particular IP address will suddenly stop working.

Dynamic Name Service (DNS)

By now you have noticed that while I claim that the Internet is built on top of IP, you can type "www.ibm.com" into a browser instead of an IP address. You can type name@domain.com as an email address. This is because someone invented Domain Name Server (DNS).

The short version is that DNS takes in names and gives back IP addresses.

The long version is that DNS is a protocol supported by a network of servers around the world. This protocol accepts a domain name as input, parses that domain name and then searches the DNS registry to see if there is a corresponding IP address.

(You will notice some basic similarities to the IP notation.)

Let us consider this example, which has the optional subdomain:

```
Sub.MyDomain.com
```

Parsing the domain goes like this:

1. Break into parts using the dots: Sub, MyDomain and com.

2. Reverse the order of the parts: com, MyDomain and Sub.

3. The first part is the Top Level Domain (TLD), in our case 'com'. [3]

4. The rest of the parts are like a directory path which, when followed, arrive at an IP host on the Internet.

This allows use to have email addresses and host names which are easier to remember than IP addresses.

Video Call Example Revisited

Now we have the tools to revisit the example in the chapter entitled *Sympathy For Tech Support*. As you may remember, my wife was trying to debug the sudden failure of a teleconferencing app with the following architecture:

1. An iPad client which provides the user interface

2. A Mac Mini server which provides the actual video call

3. The client and server communicate over a WLAN

4. The server connects to other servers over the WAN

The problem seemed to be between the client and server because the server could be used to make video calls on its own.

We can revisit this example now that we know a bit about networking:

- The client and the server have to be on the same subnet so the client can find the server. I used my iPhone to confirm that the iPad and the Mac Mini were both on the WLAN (they were).

- The server has to have a route to the WAN so that it can send and receive data across the Internet to make the video call work. I confirmed this by bringing up a public web site on the browser.

- The WLAN connects to the router which connects to the Internet. This must be working if the public web site comes up.

- I used a network protocol analyzer to show that the client was not getting a response from the server. My Protocol Analyzer is a laptop running the software called Wire Shark.

- I drafted a bug report with as much detail as was relevant and sent it off to Tech Support.

The Cloud and the Network

The Computer Cloud receives its input from the network and sends that output over the network. This means that the Cloud's public face is the network. Even though the heavy lifting is done by computers on the network, without the network there is no Cloud.

Chapter 6 End Notes

[1] Octets, being groups of eight binary digits, can only represent the values from 0 through 255.

[2] I stole this excellent analogy from a TV show I saw decades ago. I have tried and failed to find the original source to credit them. I wish I could recall the source; the visual aid was so good that I still remember it all these years later.

[3] https://en.wikipedia.org/wiki/Top-level_domain

Part III

Abstract Concepts

"A Classic--something that everybody wants to have read and nobody wants to read." Mark Twain

This part is intended to give the reader an idea of what come very commonly used terms in IT which everyone want to know about about but nobody wants to learn about.

Chapter seven is about computer data, the most common intersection of abstract and concrete. Data is mostly what all the fuss is about.

Chapter eight is about computer security, which is how we protect our data.

Chapter nine is about virtualization, which is another intersection of abstract and concrete: computers which are software running inside other computers.

Data

In this chapter, when we talk about "data" we mean what users usually mean by "data": "data external to software." We mean spreadsheets, we mean rows in databases, we mean documents, photos, videos and music files. [1]

Files & Directories

It is hard to talk about digital data without talking about computer files. And if you are talking about files, you have to talk about computer directories. And if you are talking about directories, you have to talk about subdirectories and relative paths and absolute paths. You don't really want to, but you have to.

The file-in-a-directory concept is so ingrained now that hardly anyone ever questions it. But they were not inevitable, they were a choice that we now just accept.

Imagine what it was like at the dawn of computing. Happily, the brave new virtual world of computers was rife with possibilities to help human users to comprehend it. Reasonably, the creators of this brave new world fell back on the familiar, fell back on metaphors to give this world a relatable form. Sadly, the metaphor they chose was a typical clerical office of the 1950s.

So computer data is stored in files: metaphorical memos and typewritten pieces of paper stored in metaphorical manilla folders like the physical folders so common when I was a tyke and now somewhat rare.

Mercifully, computing pioneers decided to call aggregations of files "directories" instead of "file cabinets." [2]

File Systems

Files are stored in *file systems* which is how the OS keeps track of them. File systems vary greatly in their effectiveness and reliability but that is a discussion outside the scope of this book.

What all file systems have in common is that they support the concept of "file" which has the following attributes:

FILE ATTRIBUTES

1. A name, sometimes called a "basename." For our example, because I grew up with three siblings and feel that I should never have to share anything ever again, I choose "myfile."

2. An extension [3] which, by convention, is separated from the base name by a period or dot, full-stop, the thing at the end of this sentence. If our file is a digital photograph, it might have an extension of "jpg" which would make our file name "myfile.jpg". If our file contains a document in Rich Text Format, the name would be "myfile.rtf". And so on.

3. A size, usually the length in bytes [4] or characters. [5] Mentioning bytes and characters gets into the area of data types which is not an area we want to visit. There might not be dragons there, but there are hours of explanation and the topic is beyond the scope of this book.

4. A date of most recent modification, which is self-explanatory. [6]

Directory Attributes

File systems nearly universally support the concept of directories. Directories are sort of a file cabinet, a way of grouping files (and directories) together.

1. A name, sometimes with a file extension.

2. A "parent" directory.

3. A date of most recent modification, which is the last time a file was added or removed from the directory.

4. A list of files and directories associated with this name. Any directories in this list are subdirectories of this directory and this directory is any such subdirectory's parent.

Directory Trees, aka Paths

Directories can have subdirectories; when this happens, the resulting collections of directories and subdirectories is called "a directory tree." A directory has a starting point, which is called its "root."

Just to keep it simple, let us use Unix as an example. In Unix and its children, the "separator" is the slash (also called "the forward slash") which is this: /. "/" by itself is called "root" because it is the root of all directory trees. [7]

If one were to create a subdirectory of root called "mine", then we would have created a path "/mine" in the file system because the root of a file system is represented by the "/" at start of a path.

If we created a subdirectory called "mine" (which would be confusing but perfectly legal), the path would extend to "/mine/mine" in the file system.

From that subdirectory, if we created a subdirectory called "all" that would leave a path of "/mine/mine/all" in the file system.

From that subdirectory, if we created a subdirectory called "mine" that would leave a path of "/mine/mine/all/mine" in the file system.

Every file system I have ever known supports the "change directory" command ("cd" for short) to allow users to navigate the directory tree.

ABSOLUTE PATHS

So to reach the "all" directory we could use "cd /mine/mine/all". This is called an "absolute" path because it is unambiguous and starts with root.

RELATIVE PATHS

Every file system supports the notion of "current working directory" (CWD for short) which is wherever your most recent cd left you. Since we have CWD, we can use "relative paths" which are specified relative to the CWD. Unix and Windows, at least, provide two "directory" names to aid in using relative paths: "." which is the CWD itself and ".." which specifies the parent. So if we were starting in /mine/mine/all and went to the parent (also called "up a level") with "cd .." "/mine/mine" would become our CWD.

Why Data Issues Arise

In an ideal world, you would never need to think about data: data files would never be lost, or corrupted, or forgotten or unbacked up. It would always be clear if a problem were caused by a software glitch (aka "bug") or by bad data. But this is, at least in this respect, not an ideal world.

We do want to copy our data from device to device, to access our data from different devices, to share our data with some (but not all) of the other people on the planet. In order to deal with the inevitable issues, we need to know what data is, where it comes from and where it goes.

Common Kinds of Data

There are a vast number of possible organizing principles for data stored in a computer, but generally users only run into a relatively small set of these possibilities.

Images

By "images" I mean a group of data files including electronic photos, scanned images and digital art. Images are generally accessed through a display app or an image editor. Typical file name extensions include JPEG or JPG, MPEG or MPG, GIF, PNG, IMG.

Documents

By "documents" I mean collections of words and images, usually with embedded formating to control presentation. I include presentations in this group because I find presentations functionally equivalent to documents. Typical file name extensions include DOC, DOCX, RTF.

Web Pages & Images

Web pages and any images embedded in them can be thought of as either structured text or documents or their kind of data. We will be covering web pages in their own chapter, so we will not pay much attention to them here. Documents are created and edited with word-processors.

Spreadsheets

I suppose one could argue that spreadsheets are documents, but I think of them as data sets so I put them in their own category. Spreadsheets are accessed through single-purpose software confusingly also called "spreadsheets." Just about the only spreadsheet I encounter these days is XLS; perhaps I need to get out more.

Databases

By "databases" I mean collections of data elements organized into records and accessed through a database management system. Once there were many kinds of database but now you rarely see anything but "relational" databases. Relational Databases (RDBs) are accessed through SQL, a query language which describes the world in terms of tables and rows within tables and columns within rows.

A relational database management system (RDBMS) accepts data one row at a time via SQL Insert statements, it retrieves data as a collection of rows via SQL Select statements, it changes data one row at a time via SQL Update statements and it removes data as a collection of rows via SQL Delete statements.

This is a terribly shallow overview of SQL, but for more detail you will find a chapter devoted entirely to SQL at the end of the book.

Chapter 7 End Notes

[1] Yes, I know that software has both instructions and internal data. I also know that the instructions are, themselves, data elements in some contexts. But in this context, we mean none of these things.

[2] The compulsive language nerd in me is moved to point out that this is inconsistent: directories are what these data objects are, not what these data objects represent. They should have been called file cabinets and been accessed through card catalogues. But I digress, in a vain attempt to delay writing about virtual files.

[3] Technically, in Unix-derived operating systems such as Linux or AIX, the extension is just the end of the file name. But in many other operating systems, the extension is a separate thing and that is how most people seem to think of it.

[4] A byte is an atomic unit of eight bits. "Bit" is short for "binary digit" and is capable of representing only two values: zero or one. Thanks to a British mathematician named Boole, we know that there are quite a few interesting things you can do with binary digits, which are said to be Boolean because they can only have those values.

[5] Characters, often abbreviated as "chars," are simply bytes which we intend to hold a single letter, number, piece of punctuation or other member of a "character set."

[6] Do you wish that the creation date was also always part of the overhead maintained by a file system? So do I. So do lots of people. Alas, it just is not very common.

[7] Confusingly, the most powerful user account in the Unix family of OSes is also called "root."

Computer Security

Computer Security is a huge and important topic which we will not be trying to cover here. Instead, we will cover basic concepts and associated vocabulary to facilitate conversation with IT professionals about security.

Practical Matters

There are a number of practical matters which make up "security" as most users experience it. These are the reasons that sysadmins grouse and cut off your access to email or other systems.

Specifically, most users experience computer security as a never-ending series of battles against an unseen army of foes and these battles seem to always take the form of inconveniences or scolding about clicking on this link or opening that attachment.

If you want to avoid have Tech Support grumble at you about security issues, you need to be aware of a couple of kinds of danger and follow some basic rules.

Common Attacks

There are two basic types of cyber attack: the first kind aims to plant something evil ("malware") on your network or server or client machine while the second kind aims to steal your credentials so that they can gain access to your organization's systems ("phishing").

MALWARE

Software created specifically to do something bad (and not for the user) is called "malware." Malware does things like monitor keystrokes or network traffic to steal credentials or confidential information.

Malware usually has many ways to propagate around a network or computers that have contact with each other. Some viruses are spread via USB stick or other moveable media which is why your sysadmin begs you not to bring in your devices and not to copy files around using whatever USB stick or external drive you happen to have lying around.

Some of the malware propagation strategies are stolen from the natural world and malware which uses these techniques are called "viruses" and machines which have been attacked are said to be "infected."

Before malware can spread all over a system or group of somehow connected computers, it has to gain access to your systems. Like the Vampire of lore, it has to be invited in.

This is why Tech Support gets so annoyed when you click on links you should not click on, or when you open attachments in email you should not open. Because sometimes, all too often in fact, these seemingly innocent mistakes compromise a system at a very basic level.

PHISHING

When someone asks questions without having a good reason to ask them, simply in the hopes of turning up useful or damaging information, we say that that questioner is "fishing for information" or "has gone fishing."

By analogy, when an email tries to fool you into answering questions you should not answer we call that "phishing." [1] One of the issues with phishing is that the victim is often unaware that he or she has been conned. The "not knowing" is important, because what is being stolen is usually a password which the victim would change if he or she knew that she or he had to change it.

Guidelines

You can avoid many attacks of either kind by following some simple guidelines (which you have probably already heard):

- Do not click on links in emails. If you really have to click on links in emails, make sure that you know who sent the email and why. If you do not know how to tell who sent the email, then do not click on links in emails.

- Do not enter your User IDs and passwords into forms unless you are pretty darn sure that they are the right forms, the appropriate forms, the real forms. If you do not click on links in emails, you will be presented with fewer bogus forms.

- With "two factor authentication" (two different kinds of authentication), you should be able to identify real forms by the image you have chosen or the passphrase you choose. Use two factor authentication whenever it is offered and pay attention to it.

- Do not open attachments in emails unless you know who sent the email and you are expecting the email.

- Do not accept updates by email, do not install anything (because that is not your job) and do not give any software permission to do anything unless you are utterly certain of its validity.

- Ask Tech Support when you are unsure. Either they will appreciate your caution or they will learn to communicate better to avoid the nuisance.

- Do not use USB drives (USB sticks, external drives, really anything you can easily connect and remove from computer) whose history you do not know.

- Embrace anti virus software. Run the scans. Get the updates.

Textbook Definition

So that was what security seems to be about when you are at work: preventing unauthorized access to proprietary data. But what is the textbook definition of security?

Computer Security is technically the enforcement of policies with regard to computer usage, data access and privacy invasion.

This may seem like a vague definition, but Computer Security is a notoriously large and vague topic. If you stray from this academic language you end up with definitions such as "keeping people from seeing my data unless I want them to."

Dark Security Secret #1

Security is very inconvenient. It is a nuisance. Users generally hate security because they cannot see the benefits of security, but users can see the limitations and restrictions which make users secure.

Since they are seen as the strict parents who deny all requests, security people are rarely popular. Since they are seen as useless restrictions, security measures are rarely popular. No one likes security measures or security people. But all users want to be safe.

Dark Security Secret #2

The truth is that many IT support staff are not security experts either. Security measures are often as annoying to them as they are to you. But they have to pretend to care about security even if they do not.

Physical Security

Physical Security is just what it sounds like: controlling who has access to the devices and the computers and the physical network. Physical Security generally refers to locks and keys and security guards.

Network Security

Network Security is controlling who is allowed to connect to the network and therefore all the resources on that network. Network Security generally refers to using security features of DHCP and turning on whatever security features the sources might have for security: logins, etc.

App Security

App Security generally refers to having software follow "best practices" in taking care of data, in requiring and checking user credentials.

Malware

Malware is software intended to do harm, to breach privacy rules, to transmit data, to allow access to resources outside of access policies, to corrupt or delete or steal data.

Data Security (Encryption)

Data Security generally refers to encryption, which means encoding data in a way that can be undone if you have the key.

Privacy & Snooping

Privacy is the ability to control who has access to information, but that information includes data elements not usually included in the idea of computer data:

- Your location, as transmitted by the GPS in your phone.

- Who you call and when you call them.

- What web sites you access.

- What is in your emails and with whom you exchange emails.

- Who you text and what you say in your texts.

Tools Are Neutral, People Are Not

A strange aspect of Computer Security (or security in general) is the fact that the intent of the user can determine whether or not a tool is a security problem or a debugging tool.

Examples

Just as the Fire Department has tools for breaking into cars, so software developers have tools which monitor and record computer activity. If your car has crashed and you need extraction, the tool used to rip your car open is a lifesaver. If you are asleep in bed and someone wants to steal the stereo out of your car, the tool used to rip open your locked garage is a way to break security.

If you are debugging a distributed information system, a Protocol Analyzer is a Godsend. If you are a stalker, a Protocol Analyzer is a terrible invasion of privacy.

If you are making a video call to your spouse, the camera and microphone in laptop are useful. If someone uses malware to turn them on without your knowledge, the camera and microphone in your laptop are ways to snoop.

If a medical professional engaged in your care accesses your Electronic Medical Record (EMR), then accessibility is a great boon; if that same professional accesses your EMR just for kicks, then accessibility is an issue and that access is a crime.

If you use encryption software to protect data on your laptop, then the software is helping you. If malware uses encryption software to encode data on your laptop and then charges you $300 for the encryption key, then you are the victim of "ransomware."

All About Policy After All

So Computer Security is not simply a matter of banning any software or hardware which could ever be used in a malicious way. Computer Security is about enforcing policies of access.

Chapter 8 End Notes

[1] ha! a ph instead of an f, how cute! Computer jargon generators are not exactly inventive.

Virtualization

Virtualization is the ultimate computing abstraction: the entire computer is abstracted. In other words, the virtualized computer's hardware is an app running on a physical computer, called "the host."

Thanks to the rise of the Computer Cloud, virtualization is moving from "esoteric computer topic" to "very common computing platform." And virtualization is a great example of our mantra: this works very well unless and until it does not work at all.

How It Works

How is this possible? It is actually much simpler than you might think because software can only really access hardware through RAM.

Software writes to a special chunk of RAM to make a request and reads from another special chunk of RAM.

- Want to display something? Write what is to be displayed into the chunk of RAM that is tightly coupled with the video card.

- Want to read from the hard drive? Send a request to the disk driver and read the chunk of RAM associated with the disk driver.

So if the software can only see RAM, the software cannot really know what is reading and writing that RAM. It *might* be hardware reading and writing that RAM, but it *might* be software. In other words, the Operating System (OS) might be running "on the bare metal" as we say, or the OS might be running on a virtual machine.

So a virtual machine (VM) is a piece of software which emulates hardware. The VM's OS boots in the usual way, but the "hardware" being read from and written to via RAM is actually software running on the host.

Brain In A Box

At this point, it might be helpful to consider a thought experiment from Philosophy (or the movies, [1] depending on your frame of reference).

You are somewhere in the world right now, reading this. You might be standing up in a subway in New York City or you might be sitting down on a park bench in Paris but for the sake of argument let us assume that you are sitting in a chair in your home.

Your consciousness is the result of stimuli entering your brain. This input comes in via various nerves and other connections so, in theory, you would not be able to tell if someone took your brain out of your skull and put your brain into a box, so long as the box had connections to allow someone or something to fake out those inputs. You would not be able to tell if the inputs were sufficiently well forged. In fact, perhaps your entire life could be lived that way, with you never knowing that you are "actually" a brain in a box.

So it is with virtualization: software cannot tell if the inputs it gets are from hardware or from a VM.

Layered Architecture of a VM

1. Physical hardware (the host)
2. Device drivers
3. Kernel
4. VM (which is actually an app from the host perspective)
5. Device drivers (in VM)
6. Kernel (in VM)
7. Apps (in VM)

Why Virtualization?

When it first hit the scene, in the late 1980s and early 1990s, virtualization was a specialized tool for system developers to help them develop system software: when the system software crashes in the VM environment can intercept the error and give you information about the crash. Physical hardware just...crashes. The emulation of hardware was not perfect, but it was good enough to aid in debugging. The performance was not great, but it was good enough to aid in debugging.

As time marched on, the emulation of hardware became better and better and the performance also improved because physical hardware became literally thousands of times faster. Once the emulation became good enough to trust and fast enough to use, virtualization moved out of the lab and into the field.

As virtualization moved into the mainstream, sysadmins found a multitude of uses for it. Here are some of the most common uses I have encountered:

Economy of Scale

As the price per cycle has dropped, it has become cheaper to buy computing power but companies no longer need one or two giant computers: companies generally need dozens of medium-sized computers. With virtualization, you can buy a giant computer and have it run dozens of VMs.

Uptime (aka Availability)

VMs can greatly increase the amount of time that a computer service is up, or available. VMs increase uptime in at least three scenarios.

BACKING UP

Some VM environments can trap the VM's requests to write to the disk so that the VM is backed up as it goes along, meaning that there does not need to be any downtime to back up.

CHAPTER 9   *Virtualization*   73

RANSOMWARE ANTIDOTE

If you are running a VM which is automatically backed up, then if ransomware strikes, you shrug and go back to your most recent checkpoint that does not have the ransomware on it yet and restart the VM from that checkpoint. So you ignore the ransom request. And even go through checkpoints and logs to find out how the ransomware was introduced onto your system.

Legacy App Support

Apps often have short useful lifespans, but some have very long lifespans. When an app remains in service for a long time, the physical hardware becomes out-of-date and hard to support. It is often easier to support an older app with a VM which emulates out-of-date hardware.

Sometimes legacy apps require a particular or peculiar configuration which no other app needs; with VMs, you can have that configuration only on the server which needs it.

There is even software to "virtualize" a physical machine to create a VM from it, so "retiring" a physical server as a VM means continuity of service to the users even if the legacy server is no longer supportable.

Virtualization and Users

As we have seen, virtualization can be a boon to users, providing the experience of local servers at lower price, or extending the useful life of apps even after those apps no longer have a physical host.

But virtualization is often utterly baffling for end users because sys admin often do not even tell end users that the end users are interacting with VMs and physical hardware. So if and when something goes awry in the VM or its environment, the end user does not even know that the VM is there, let alone how to describe how it has failed.

In particular, if the host needs to be worked on, end users are often unable to understand why their perfectly functional server (which is actually a VM) has to be shut down (and might disappear entirely!).

Virtualization and the Cloud

The services which define the Cloud are often provided by VMs because VMs allow the administrators of the Cloud to provide a wide range of services without having to have an army of physical machines. VMs can be called into existence in response to demand. VMs can make billing easier too, if there is one VM per client.

Chapter 9 End Notes

[1] Both "The Matrix" and "Inception" borrowed heavily from this thought experiment.

Part IV

System Administration

This part is about System Administration: what it is and why we need it (and why it is so often only seen as an impediment to getting work done).

Chapter ten is an overview of system administration and what system administrators (sysadmins) do for a living.

Chapter eleven is about Back Up & Recovery which is a part of system administration that no one cares about until they need it. Backing up is often annoying in that backing up often interrupts operations. Recovery is often nail-biting as you wait for the restoration of missing or corrupted data.

Chapter twelve is a round-up of system administration tasks which are often lumped under "network administration" or "netadmin."

System Administration

We give System Administration its own chapter because so much of the friction between users and the keepers of IT (Tech Support or sysadmin) arises because sysadmins enforce policy and policy rarely makes non-IT operations smoother or easier.

I thought that the Wikipedia definition was as good or better than I could do, so I am just going to refer to it:

A system administrator, or sysadmin, is a person who is responsible for the upkeep, configuration, and reliable operation of computer systems; especially multi-user computers, such as servers.

System administrator - Wikipedia

```
en.wikipedia.org/wiki/System_administrator
```

Sysadmin Areas of Responsibility

In practice, the sysadmin's job generally covers these areas:

Uptime / Downtime

"Uptime" is the amount of time per unit (day, month, year, depending on context) that a computer system is available to users. By analogy, "downtime" is the opposite: the amount of time per unit that a computer system not available to users.

Downtime can be "scheduled" or "unscheduled." Neither is popular with users but the latter is especially unwelcome.

Configuration

Apps often have options which control and customize their operations. Some of these options are mostly cosmetic, e.g. the colors of various elements on the screen. Some of these options are used to customize the app's operations to better fit the local business processes and policies.

CHAPTER 10   *System Administration*

Configuration is often complicated by these factors:

NUMBER OF OPTIONS

I have worked with Commercial Off-the-Shelf (COTS) software with over 1,500 user-settable options. I assert that this many possible interactions is beyond human comprehension.

LAYERS UPON LAYERS

I have worked with COTS software which was configurable in different layers. By this I mean that there are different configuration pathways which are at more or fewer removes from the app itself.

Typically, the lowest layer is low-level configuration files, which were designed to be easy for software to read, not easy for human beings to write.

In theory, all the layers do the same thing. In practice, configuration layers are like paint on a window sill: the more layers of paint you apply, the less underlying detail you can discern. Often each successive layer of configuration software fails to layer (all too often because the author of the higher level does not know or does not care about the unsupported options). Since higher level configuration tools hide or obscure options, a user who knows how to access and control one of the lower layers can do "magic" things which are simply not possible for users of higher levels.

Programmers were generally happy to write these files, but non-programmers balked, so someone wrote a nicer User Interface (UI-1) to read in these files, present the user with options, and write out any changes into the original configuration file format.

Often Tech Support decides that UI-1 is still too geeky, or still offers too many options, many of which non-programmers don't even understand, let alone want to change. So someone else writes UI-2 which is easier to use, partly because it does not expose everything.

Then, as the software matures and becomes better understood, marketing will want something for "super users," for the customer who *really* wants control. And UI-3 is born, sort of a cross between

UI-1 and UI-2.

After a while, users at new installations are horrified to find they are shown UI-2 but cannot seem to do everything that Tech Support can do. And sometimes, for reasons not clear to the end user, Tech Support has to escalate the end user's issue all the way to the programmers, who simply fiddle with the configuration file directly and something impossible happens.

In fact, new users may see UI-3 at installation time because it is "the one for users" and "the easiest one to use." But UI-3 does not do everything, so users will be asked to use UI-2 when dealing with front-line Tech Support, who know more than users but less than experts. If their problem is "escalated" beyond front-line Tech Support, users may be forced to suffer through UI-1 on the phone with Tech Support old-timers (who know nothing else) or experts (who need the functionality). At the most extreme end of the scale, poor old end users may even be talked through making the occasional fix to the configuration files directly, using a text file editor, an experience that generally either terrifies users or gives them dangerous delusions of power. No wonder even reasonable people sometimes give up on configuration and leave it to the experts.

Backup & Recovery

Backup and Recovery are two sides of the same coin. Many people think of Backup as a separate thing, but what is the point of a backup if you cannot restore from it? Backup & Recovery is a big topic that it gets its own chapter.

Preventive Maintenance

Most computer systems, like most domiciles, require a bit of housekeeping. We call the housekeeping that we can schedule "preventive maintenance." Typical PM tasks include backing up data and configurations, deleting temporary files, "rotating" logs [1], restarting servers to give them a clean slate, etc.

Security

Increasingly, security has its own group within IT but often that security group sets policy but leaves implementation to the sysadmins.

Security for sysadmins often centers on access to resources: who can access what, who can print, who can bring their devices into work, etc.

User Credentials

User credentials are sort of configuration and sort of security. Sysadmins are usually charged with creating user accounts (new hires), updating user accounts (promotion, demotion, transfer), or deleting user accounts (terminations and resignations).

Occupational Hazard

Sysadmins often get a bad rap because their job is to make systems as reliable as possible; in fact, sysadmins are now often called "System Reliability Engineers" or "SREs".

Nanny Sysadmin

In order to maximize uptime, SREs often try to restrict what software can be installed, or what configuration options can be set, or what kinds of devices can be brought to work. This kind of apparently arbitrary restriction can often hurt the popularity of sysadmins.

Scheduling PM

Users tend to want PM scheduled for late at night or on the weekends. Sysadmins tend to prefer having personal time. Unless your organization is big enough to run a night shift, scheduling PM is another source of sysadmin unpopularity.

Roles & Policies

Enforcing job descriptions (roles to the software) and enforcing policies often puts sysadmins in the position of enforcing the "official" reality even if the actual reality is different. For example, sysadmins are supposed to keep assistants from using their boss' credentials even if their bosses explicitly demand it. Often users shoot the messenger, blaming the sysadmin for the annoying (and secure) policy that seems only to get in the way of getting work done.

Chapter 10 End Notes

[1] Sysadmins love logs but they love disk space more; the typical compromise is to keep the logs by day and then keep 30 days's worth. If you keep four logs, then today's log might be "my.log" and yesterday's would be "my.log.0" and the next day's would be "my.log.1" and the earliest of the four would be "my.log.2". But tomorrow is a new day and brings a new log, so the oldest log is deleted and then the other logs are "rotated": my.log.1 -> my.log.2; my.log.0 -> my.log.1; my.log -> my.log.0 and then a new "my.log" is created.

Backup & Recovery

Backup and Recovery are two sides of the same coin. Many people think of Backup as a separate thing, but what is the point of a backup if you cannot restore from it?

When you make a backup, you have to do these things:

1. Select files or records or other kinds of data to be backed up
2. Convert the selected data in an archive format
3. Copy the archived data onto some kind of storage medium

(If you are running a VM, you might be able to make a snapshot which is an image of the running VM at some point in time.)

In order to recover from disaster, you would be wise to keep at least some of your backups somewhere else ("offsite").

Kinds Of Failure

There are three main kinds of IT failure from which one might wish to recover:

1. **Human error**: deleting by accident, regretted edit, etc. In this case, the selection is relatively straightforward and specific: the files you changed or lost.

2. **Hardware failure**: hard disk failure, etc. In this case, the selection can be tricky: all the data lost to the failure; perhaps a full restore is the best bet.

3. **Disaster**: flood, fire, power outage, etc. In this case, first you need to recreate the host computer. Which might be quite tricky unless you have a system backup or perhaps you were using a VM, in which case recreating is easy (or using a snapshot is even better).

Backup Trade Offs

When backing up, you face a backing up trade-off: time (how long the back up takes) versus space (how much storage is used by the file or files created by the backup). You also face a recovery trade-off: ease of backing up versus ease of restoring whatever was lost.

Ideally you do backups many times a day, to provide good coverage. Practically there is a huge drawback: when you do backups frequently it often interferes with normal operations, so users can get cranky.

So in the usual case there is pressure to make backups less frequently. Backups are healthy habits and good hygiene of the tech world.

But restoring data is the first aid of the tech world. Restoring is usually done under pressure, sometimes under great pressure with users freaking out about their lost data.

So you can be lulled into thinking that backing up is a tedious chore--unless and until you need to restore, in which case you will wish that there were great and frequent backups. Rather like finding out that you have a cavity and wishing you had brushed more often.

How do you balance the backup process with the restore process? Concretely, what kind of backup should you do? That depends on your situation.

Kinds of Backup

Now that we know the trade-offs in general, let us consider the specific options:

- The most obvious kind of backup is the **full backup**. As the time implies, it is a backup of all the system's data: [1] it takes the most time and the most space, so it is the most expensive kind of backup, but your best friend when it is time to restore something.

- If you do not mind making restoration more complicated, you can make infrequent full backups and then do frequent **incremental backups** which select all the files changed since the last full backup.

- If you have a VM, you can get a **snap shot**, which is a complete image of what the VM was doing when the snap shot was made.

Recovery

For too many sysadmins, recovering data is much like the lob:

The lob, much like prayer, is seldom practiced except in times of need. (Old tennis adage)

When you recover data, you have to do these things:

1. Find the archive you want (ideally using an index of the archive)
2. Find the associated storage medium
3. Select files or records to restore
4. Run the restore software, which will search the archive
5. Extract the selected files from the archive and write them to disk

What Can Go Wrong

This all sounds simple enough, but there are potential issues in recovery:

- Selecting files can go wrong, in which case you risk restoring out-of-date versions of records or files on top of newer (presumably better) versions.

- Finding the right archive from which to restore can go wrong, in that you either waste time looking for what is not there or you restore the wrong version of the files or records.

- When you extract from an archive, you need to put the extracted records or files somewhere. Sometimes you want to restore to a scratch area, to compare and confirm; sometimes you want to restore back to the extract path that was backed up. Just about every recovery app can do either. Choosing the option which is *not* the option you want can be very unfortunate.

Kinds of Recovery

- If you have deleted a file by accident, or changed something you wish you had not changed, you would want to get the file back. We make nightly backups of our user files by day going back five days, so if we delete a file and discover it within five days, selection and unarchiving is pretty straightforward.

- If you have a hardware failure, you would want to replace the hardware and restore the entire disk from backup.

- If you have a disaster, you would want to get a new machine, install the system software you were using and then restore the entire file system from backup.

Chapter 11 End Notes

[1] Full backups often cannot backup the parts of the system in use by the backup program, alas.

Users, Printers, Servers & Shares

When people think of the networks they usually think of the resources accessed over the network. We speak of "logging into the network" and "accessing the network" but we usually mean "logging into a user authentication server" and "accessing servers on the network."

Sysadmins' most visible responsibilities are Printers, Servers, Shares and Users.

Users

Once upon a time, in the mainframe era, user authentication was done on a server-by-server basis, or on an app-by-app basis.

Then came the PC era and we tried to reconcile the user model of the PC (the user rules) and the user model of the server (the user must be authenticated). In order to bridge these two very different ideas, the concept of the user authentication server was invented. "User authentication server" was too much to say, so people started saying "the network" instead, hence "network login" or "login to the network" or "network administration" meaning user accounts instead of routing or IP addressing.

Once we had the network user concept, it was a relatively small leap to making servers "trust" the network user credentials and give up local authentication, so logging into the network allows the user to use the servers, printers and shares.

Then came the Web era with the need for users to access web apps, sometimes across web apps. In an attempt to enhance the user experience, we tried to map the network login concept to the web application arena. This was a far more catch-as-catch-can process since web servers are sometimes part of the local organization and sometimes web servers are remote and yet both are equally accessible by the users.

In the MS-Windows world, the original user authentication server is the built-in Microsoft User Administration subsystem. Later came the Active Directory (AD) protocol and implementation. AD was aimed at enterprise-wide user management in a way that User

Administration was not.

In the Unix world, the original user authentication was the built-in user authentication system which was extended to be shared across specially configured Unix servers. As time went on, inter-operability with MS-Windows went from fringe to mainstream and support for AD was added so that Unix servers could participate in MS-Windows-based networks and accept print jobs from PCs and share files with PCs.

When this all works, this distributed authentication system, it is an enormous convenience. You sign in once at the beginning of your workday and all day long you transparently have access to printers, to servers and shares. When it does not work, distributed authentication is both difficult to debug and essential to debug quickly. Not a combination that makes for easy relations between netadmin and user.

Printers

Although our reliance on paper is starting to decline, many of us still need to generate physical pages as part of our job. Desktop printers are great for execs who print out the occasional short and possibly confidential document, but for most uses the networked printer is the way to go. A large, fast, reliable printer which is accessible from anywhere on the network is a common networked resource. Once the network login concept came into vogue, printers with built-in printer servers became the most common kind of shared network resource.

When the printing fails there are many possible sources of error:

- the user permissions for using the printer

- the network connectivity between PC and networked printer

- the printer itself (paper, toner, ink,)

- the embedded printer server (wedged, needing a reboot)

Servers

There are three basic kinds of server which are neither printers nor users: file servers, database servers and web servers.

File Servers

File Servers provide access to files across the network, assuming that the user access policies are met. File servers make system administration easier: users can share files but sysadmins can take responsibility for backing up the file server and controlling access to the files.

Shares

When file servers can appear to be a "drive" on an MS-Windows PC or a mounted file system on a Unix box, we call that a "shared drive" or "share" for short. Or "network share" for slightly longer than short.

Database Servers

When a Database Management System (DBMS) is on a server and accepts requests for data over the network and returns the data over the network, then the server is a Database Server. Database servers are just like file servers except that they manage records instead of files; the same benefits apply.

Web Servers

We will cover web servers in a bit more detail in the chapter on HTML, but this quick overview will suffice for now.

A web server is a server which is running the Hyper Text Transport Protocol (HTTP), which was created to allow servers to serve up HTML and images. Web servers were created to allow the quick and easy sharing of scientific papers and the security model was very lax: if you can find a web page, you can view it. The assumption was that the information being served up was public, or if private, then protected by network configuration to be reachable only by users who are allowed to see it. This open model is very hard to map onto the network login model, but people have done it with varying degrees of success.

When the network configuration is wrong, or the jury-rigged user authentication is wrong, or the user authentication is not properly shared by all the software you use, then web-based resources can seem broken or mis-configured.

Part V

Development & Deployment

This part is about software development and deployment. It is intended to give you some insight into why software so often seems to get worse as time goes by. It is also intended to help you make bug reports to sysadmins or Tech Support.

Chapter thirteen is a general overview of programming languages; it is intended to make talking to IT folks a bit easier and understanding their tools a bit easier in the hope that understanding the tools will help you understand the results.

Chapter fourteen is about how new versions of existing software can be a mixed blessing. Specifically, this chapter is about releases, updates and upgrades.

Chapter fifteen is about how to make a bug report which is easier for Tech Support to read and act upon.

Programming Language Overview

When all you have is a hammer, everything looks like a nail

Why is there a section on programming languages in a book for non-programmers? The short answer is that a programmer's tools can have a big impact on the apps they produce. Having a basic idea of what the options are might be helpful when talking to IT people about IT or even when struggling to use IT itself.

What This Chapter Is Not

In order to avoid confusion or disappointment, here is a list of what this chapter is not:

- A tutorial on programming itself

- An explanation of the software development process

- A critique of programming languages in particular

That last point is important: different programmers have different strengths and weaknesses and different programming languages have different attributes. Thus programmers are often a better fit for some programming languages and a worse fit for other programming languages. Programmers tend to call the first group "better" and the second group "worse." Arguments about the relative merits of different programming languages with programmers who lack a deep self-awareness is, to quote Twain, like trying to teach a pig to sing: it doesn't work and annoys the pig.

Basic Programming Language Model

So what is a programming language? How does it produce software? How does a particular programming language influence the final product?

In the simplest terms, a human being writes source code in the programming language and then the source code is translated into machine code for the computer to execute.

Layered Architecture of Programming Languages

1. Hardware (or the VM)

2. Machine code (the instructions native to the CPU)

3. System software (low level software to support apps)

4. Software source code (what the human wrote)

Implementation: Compiled vs Interpreted vs Hybrid

Some programming languages are *compiled* which means that the source code is translated into machine code in one step and the machine code package is a stand-alone program which is executed. The C programming language is one of these.

Some programming languages are *interpreted* which means that the source code is run through an interpreter which compiles and executes it one statement at a time. The BASIC programming language is one of these.

Some programming languages are *pseudo-compiled* which means that the source code is compiled into pseudo code ("pcode") and that pcode is executed by a pcode interpreter. The Java programming language is one of these.

What Difference Does It Make?

In theory, the programming language used does not determine the final product. In practice the programming language can make quite a difference.

Some general observations:

Compiled languages tend to produce compact executables. Interpreted languages tend to have more features because they can use the features of the underlying interpreter.

Compiled languages require more effort to "build" the app but can be better tailored to a specific environment. Interpreted languages require much less effort to get running as they start with a working program (the interpreter).

Compiled languages tend to be better for system software, since they *can* produce smaller, cleaner, more reliable programs. Interpreted languages tend to be better for user applications, since they *can* produce more feature-filled and consistent-with-other-apps User Interfaces.

Some more specific observations follow.

Portability

The ability to move an app from one environment to another is called "portability." This was more important back in the day when running on many platforms was more important. Now, with the rise of the Client/Server model, portability often does not matter as much as it used to. The rise of VM means that packaging up an app with its server and its system software and its virtual hardware is relatively easy.

But some kinds of apps really need to be portable, such as the software that runs the VM.

Performance

The speed with which software performs its appointed task or tasks is call "performance." Performance is the complex interplay of the following attributes:

- How efficiently software does its job

- How big the executable image is

- How well the software interfaces with the host system

- How much RAM the software consumes

The compiled languages tend to be better along each of these dimensions and therefore tend to produce better performance.

Note: for many user apps, performance is not an issue.

Maintainability

The level of effort required to fix bugs and make changes to software is called "maintainability." Common factors in maintainability are these:

- How well organized the software is
- How much code there is to maintain
- How hard it is to build, ship and install an upgrade

The interpreted environments tend to be better along each of these dimensions and therefore tend to produce easier to maintain software.

Reliability

The reliability of technology is a very concrete concept: it is the number of operations or iterations technology can perform without an error or fault. In this context "error or fault" means an unexpected output for a given input. [1]

Reliability can be better for interpreted languages because less of the app is new and more of it is the (presumably) tried-and-true interpreter.

No matter how technology is produced, reliability has to be baked in and part of the engineering from day one. So it matters who did the software engineering and how they did it more than what tool they used.

Features

What software can do is called its "feature set" and the individual attributes themselves are called "features."

Compiled languages tend to offer fewer 'native' features while interpreted languages tend to offer a larger number of 'native' features.

Note: having lots of features is not necessarily a good thing. In fact, excess features accruing over time ('feature bloat') is a problem with more mature apps. You want the right feature set more than just lots of features.

Conclusion

What you really want is reliable software with a complete feature set. But when that is not what you get, at least now you should be able to understand some of the jargon you get in the excuses.

Chapter 13 End Notes

[1] Some people prefer measuring the error rate, the number of errors per some number of operations, such as errors per thousand operations.

Software Releases, Updates & Upgrades

Some of the most feared phrases in IT are these:

- "That will be fixed in the next release."

- "There is a mandatory security update to be installed."

- "This upgrade will give the app a whole new look."

To be fair, Tech Support is just like every other kind of support service: you only notice it when it does not work perfectly. There are many releases which quietly fix problems without drawing attention to themselves. There are lots of updates which provide a benefit without causing chaos. There are legions of upgrades which actually bring the improvements they promise. But too many releases, updates and upgrades draw attention to themselves in unwanted ways.

That is why people are snarky about "constant" changes to their smart phones. And people are frustrated with how often their laptops reboot themselves with a seemingly endless stream of updates and upgrades.

In order to understand how these unhappy events occur, we need a quick detour through the software development process (or at least a simplified version).

Software Development

Software Development is not quite like anything else I have done or watched being done.

It is like engineering, except that the "material" being engineered is nearly infinitely malleable.

It is like architecture, except that developers also build the "buildings" after (and sometimes as) we design them.

It is like creative writing, except that the audience is an automaton who doesn't like or dislike the text but faithfully executes it.

It is like creating a recipe except that you don't prepare the food, instead it is prepared by a robot who mindlessly obeys and doesn't eat.

Scale

Scale is a huge factor in how the various aspects of software development play out. Perhaps a set of interlocking analogies will give you a sense of the range of software development tasks and environments.

AGILE

The current new thing in software development is the agile team. The ideal agile teams focus on the immediate, work in small cross-functional teams, move fast and break stuff (to quote the founder of Facebook).

The agile team is agile because it should have most of the answers it needs (by virtue of being cross-functional) and because it is assigned a small, discrete task and because it is focused on that task. The agile team codes, tests and releases as quickly as possible.

The agile teams are kept on track by the project manager, who uses whatever task-management methodology they like .(Kanban is very popular choice among agile practitioners).

The agile teams are coordinated and directed by the product owner, who deeply understands the product at the engineering level and understands the needs of the business stake holders.

Scale is not a big issue because it is relatively easy to find more people to make more teams.

The problem the agile team was created to solve was long lead times for fixes and features. And the tyranny of designers and coding teams. And lack of input from outside voices until late in the process.

CHAPTER 14 *Software Releases, Updates & Upgrades* 97

WATERFALL

The traditional software development model is called "waterfall."

At the low end of the scale we have the archetypal "boy in the basement" who bangs out a smart phone app and makes his fortune; that loner is more like a craftsman than a bricklayer.

In the middle of the scale lies the programmer who is part of a small team creating a software unit; such a team member is more like an engineer than an architect.

At the high end of the scale, the member of a large team who executes her small part of a large design is more like a bricklayer than an engineer.

At the very high end of the scale is the designer of a large app is more like an architect than a contractor.

The project manager of software system is more like a contractor than a craftsman.

WATERFALL DEVELOPMENT CYCLE

Software is developed in an iterative process, in a feedback loop which is probably already somewhat familiar to you.

1. Identify a problem or task
2. Design a software solution
3. Write source code to implement that design
4. Quality Assurance (testing)
5. Fix the bugs and shortcomings uncovered by testing
6. Retest the patched, updated or upgraded software
7. Document what you have done
8. Distribute and deploy the product

9. Gather feedback from users, return to the "Fix the bugs" step

Fast or Safe

In theory, either process should produce a linear march toward perfection. In practice, the progress is not so linear.

The reasons are simple enough, even if their interplay is not.

- Users are not a monolith: they are a mosaic with competing priorities and clashing expectations

- Making changes is relatively easy; validating changes is relatively hard. Making sure that the sum total of all the changes made by lots of programmers to lots of lines of code all work together as intended is very hard.

- Releasing software is quite a bit of effort so it is rarely worth it to make small, safe changes. So there is a real tension between trying to move safely and trying to move quickly.

Agile, Lean, Fast & Safe?

Supposedly, the Agile methodology and the Lean approach give you fast and safe, by allowing the team to focus on getting working code out the door while ignoring useless bureaucracy. I have worked on a few projects which use these ideas and with a couple of different teams and have yet to be convinced that this is the silver bullet of software development and deployment, but who knows? In a few years we may be awash in cheaper, properly featured and more reliable software. Wouldn't that be great?

(I thought that *The Lean Startup* was worth reading, but it did not change my life; however, it seems to have changed other peoples' lives so if you are interested in how Lean is supposed to work, perhaps you should check it out.)

Look & Feel

Conceptually, software has a "front end" (User Interface) and a "back end" (the part that does the work requested through the UI). Users rarely know or care what the back end does and focus heavily on the front end. So new versions are often viewed by users through the lens of what matters to them, not what the software does.

The user experience is often called "look-and-feel." Users are very sensitive to look-and-feel; often what determines how major a new version seems is how much it changes the look-and-feel.

Why So Many New Versions?

A question I am often asked is why? Why so many new versions? Here are the most common reasons I see:

- New features: users keep asking for new features, or new ways to access the existing features.

- Bugs in the app: fixing things wrong with the app.

- Changes in the system software: sometimes you have to change your app because the underlying system software has been changed or debugged.

- Tech Support changes: sometimes Tech Support needs additional logging or some other debugging information.

Releases

Software versions are packaged up into releases; releases are what are distributed by the software producers to the software consumers. Releases are what are downloaded and installed and run.

Some producers prefer to use a regular release schedule, packaging up whatever is ready on a monthly or quarterly basis. Others prefer to release when there is a good reason. There are "major" releases and "minor" releases.

Some producers use the version number as the major number and the release-with-version as the minor number. Others up the version number only when the changes are drastic.

In a sane world, the release is relatively well-defined, so you know what you get if you accept it / download it / install it. A release is an administrative unit and often has less to do with the payload (update or upgrade or bug fixes) and more to do with whatever was ready to go when the cutoff came. Many source code control systems package up releases automatically which is why release numbers are often so ugly.

It is not natural to notice or care about the release date or exact version number of the software you are using, but as we will see in the next chapter, learning to find and report the exact version will make it easier for Tech Support to help you.

Updates

When the level of changes is low enough, you have an update. Sometimes the update does not make much difference that the user can see; none the less, much has changed. Sometimes the update does not change much other than the User Interface but this is what the users often notice.

Updates should be relatively safe to install and relatively unlikely to change the look-and-feel.

Updates often are concentrated on the back end where end users are not as likely to notice them. Updates are often aimed at Sysadmins and Tech Support, to make software stabler or easier to administrate.

Upgrades

A software upgrade is a version of software which adds a feature or features, which materially changes the look-and-feel.

This glorious simple definition leaves out all the attributes which strike terror in the hearts of so many users.

CHAPTER 14   *Software Releases, Updates & Upgrades*   101

When they work as planned, upgrades are barely noticeable except for the new feature or features.

In all cases other than glorious success, you will need some vocabulary and some concepts to comprehend the issues.

Stability (Instability)

The stability of software is a measure of how difficult it is to cause the software to fail. Stability generally takes time to build up in code base, as more and more obscure bugs are found and fixed. Major releases (upgrades) often bring instability along with their major changes.

The Perfect Bug Report

In many ways this chapter is the point of this book: how to ask Tech Support for help in a way that is efficient and effective.

In this chapter I will be using the first person much more than I have previously or will again because in this chapter I am using my personal experience as the voice on the other end of the line, from my time as software developer, a programming team leader, a software designer and a senior executive at a software firm making emergency Tech Support visits and talking to senior executives at large customer sites.

In my experience, bad bug reports are the biggest source of friction between users and Tech Support. Learning to make better bug reports can greatly improve your relationship with Tech Support and IT.

The Help Desk

The first step on your bug reporting Odyssey is often the Help Desk. Their job is twofold: to protect me from you and your potential to waste my time and to take your input and fashion it into the perfect bug report. Ideally with the duplicates weeded out. And assigned a "ticket number" so I can keep track of what is on my plate and what is already done.

The Perfect Bug Report

In a nutshell, the good bug report is just like a good newspaper article in that it follows the five W's: who, what, where, why, when.

The Five W's

- *Who* had this problem? User accounts can have different configurations and it sometimes matters which user had the problem.

- *What* went wrong? This requires that you tell us what *should* have happened as well as what *actually* happened. In this day and age of cell phone cameras and screen grabs and screen snapshots, you should almost always be able to show us exactly what happened.

- *Where* were you in the software? How would I recreate your failure if I need to?

- *When* is the easiest but for some reason the rarest piece of information we get. When you have to wade through thousands of lines of logging, it is *really* nice to know pretty exactly when the problem happened. Even if sometimes I do not need this information.

- *Why* are you telling me this now? In other words, what is the priority of this issue and why is it important? I am weary of being told that every problem is the top priority.

This sounds simple enough, so how does making a bug report go so badly so very often?

In order to better understand how to make a perfect bug report, we are going to take a turn down the dark alley of terrible bug reports.

Bad Bug Reports

Good bug reports provide a clear and accurate description of the unexpected or undesired behavior, with enough context to allow a reasonable technologist to diagnose the problem, which means first understanding the problem, reproducing the problem and researching the problem.

Bad bug reports fail on at least one and sometimes several of these fronts. Worse, a bad bug report can send you down a rat hole of the wrong behavior or off into the weeds of looking at the wrong part of the system.

The Wrong Foot

When making a bug report, users often get off on the wrong foot from the very start. IT is pervasive in most current workplaces and often essential to most current jobs. When IT works as expected, IT is almost invisible. When IT fails to work as expected, users can get pretty frustrated pretty quickly. Frustrated people are rarely cordial and clear and even rarer is the person who knows that their frustration is making them unpleasant.

Asymmetrical Relationship

Saying that frustrated users are often unpleasant and unclear is not to say that Tech Support does not attract more than its fair share of socially maladroit personalities. But the typical Tech Support's frequent brusqueness does not mean that being rude to them is effective. Ideally, Tech Support would also work hard to be better communicators and more pleasant in their demeanors. But they do not have to learn to be nicer in order to do their jobs while you may have to learn to be clearer in order to do your job.

Vague & Negative

The bad bug report can be summed up in this slight exaggeration: "Something somewhere went wrong." The short version is "it didn't work." For extra annoying qualities, you can add "and it hasn't been working for months."

The bad bug report does not tell me anything that I need to know. It makes me do all the work. Even if I am eager to help and yearning to fix whatever is wrong, I do not enjoy starting from scratch and then trying to get all the data I need.

The bad bug report does not let me get down to work trying to understand the problem, then reproducing the problem and then researching a solution. Remember, once I make sense of your bug report, my job has often only just begun; making sense of a bug report is usually merely the prelude to the to hard work of debugging.

Debugging: The End Goal

From your end, a perfect bug report gives me the five W's as well as the relevant software version and release and release date. So what do I do with your bug report and why do I need all that detail?

Classify the Issue

The first thing I need to do is figure out what kind of issue is being reported.

A Bug

When the software's response to legal input is not as defined, then you have a bug: a flaw, an error, a mistake to be corrected. This is the simplest case and the one hardest on the software producer's ego.

CRASHING

If the software session terminates by any means other than an explicit exit command, the software has "crashed."

HANGING

If the UI "freezes" and stops reacting to the user's input, but the software session does not end, then the software has "frozen."

SPINNING

If the software keeps running, consuming CPU cycles and RAM, but not responding to the user's input, then the software is "spinning" or "a zombie."

FRONT END BUG

If the UI does not behave in a consistent manner, many users will be confused or irritated. Some people claim that documenting bad behavior magically changes a bug into a feature. These people are often very unpopular.

BACK END BUG

If the UI behaves as expected but the software does not react sanely to the UI's input, then we have a back end bug. Some back end bugs are notable for the awkward way the software handles them, causing the program to crash with a cryptic error message.

CORE DUMP

If a software session goes badly enough, the system software sometimes terminates the session itself and writes out the software session's RAM image as a file which can be examined later with debugging tools.

User Confusion

When things do not go as the user expects, sometimes the problem is with the user's expectations. For example, "I could not enter 'BX012' in the Zip code" is not a bug in the software, it is a bug in the user's expectations.

Enhancement In Disguise

To continue with the Zip code example, perhaps the user really meant to request an enhancement: "please upgrade the software to support non-US postal addresses."

It is a common source of irritation for software producers that users are constantly trying to sneak in enhancements under the "bug" heading.

It is a common source of irritation for software consumers that bug reports always have much higher priority than enchancement requests.

But if I can cast the bug report as a stealth enhancement request, I can often get it off my list and onto someone else's list. Not the most satisfying way to get something off the list, but a way none-the-less.

A Repeatable Case

The second thing I do is try to establish a repeatable case. Once we have repeatability, I can use any tools in a pretty powerful tool kit for monitoring running processes. A repeatable case is the Holy Grail of debugging.

Forensic Investigation

If I do not have a repeatable case, then I have to get forensic. I have to hope that there are traces in logs and core dumps and the like. This is not nearly as easy a task as using a repeatable case.

Part VI

HTML, SQL & XML

This part is a bonus for readers who want to know more about three non-programming languages which crop up frequently in current IT.

Chapter sixteen is about HTML, the language of the World Wide Web, and the technology which serves up and renders HTML documents.

Chapter seventeen is about SQL, the language of database access. Since SQL is a linguistic interface, it is something that end users sometimes see and quite probably can understand.

Chapter eighteen is about XML, the language often used to move data from one computer system or app to another computer system or app.

HTML Overview

HTML stands for "Hyper-Text Markup Language."

Hyper-Text

Hyper-Text is text that allows linking between arbitrary bits of text and other bits of arbitrary text. In theory this linking allows deep structures in the text to be made explicit, and allows the reader to control their journey through the text.

The dream was to allow non-linear narratives and help usher in a new era of Post Modern literature.

The reality is that we now have a relatively easy-to-use, almost global pipeline for relatively easy-to-produce content. The ability to link to related or relevant content can make a document vastly more useful and interesting. This inter-connectedness, when it is done well, can be compelling and mesmerizing. That is why "surfing the web" can be such a huge consumer of time.

Markup Language

Markup Language is a technical term which harkens back to the old days of publishing when "marking up" meant "specifying how to format the text." In the computer world, "Markup Language" means a structured text format for specifying how a document should be defined.

In practice, these days Markup Languages are almost all sets of tags in angle brackets. For example a "this" tag would look like <this>.

Tags are closed with a close tag. The close tag is just like the open tag, except that the close tag starts with "/" like </this>. So a "this" tag with the contents "contents" would look like "<this>contents</this>."

The standard in the publishing world is Standard Generalized Markup Language (SGML). SGML is a way to define a structured document language, but for some reason the guy who defined

HTML did not use SGML. He did use the tag format and borrowed a vague sense of structured document. (Later other people went back and did much of the work that was not done in the first iteration.)

So HTML is, literally, a pretty simple document specification language. But HTML is often shorthand for the entire technology stack which drives "the world wide web" (known as "WWW" or "the web" for short). So let us take a quick detour to the web to frame the description of HTML.

The World Wide Web

The Internet is a collection of computers (hosts) which are physically connected through the "Internet Backbone" and virtually connected through the Internet Protocol (IP).

The IP was created to be the basis on which higher level protocols are built. One such protocol is the Hyper-Text Transport Protocol (HTTP). This protocol defines requests for "resources" (text and images) and responses to those requests.

URLs

The resources are described or defined by a Universal Resource Locator (URL). [1]

The anatomy of a URL is pretty simple:

{protocol}://{domain name}/{path to resource}

So this is a URL for a resource named "myfile.html" which is found in "mydir" on the computer named "www" in the domain "mydomain.com":

```
http://www.mydomain.com/mydir/myfile.html
```

This is the usual case we see: HTTP protocol and a web server named "www" in the domain.

This is also a URL: [2]

```
ftp://user:password@www.mydomain.com/mydir/myfile.html
```

This URL has the ancient and venerable File Transfer Protocol as the protocol. FTP, while deprecated, at least requires a user ID and a password. Which probably become sadly insecure once you put them in a URL.

HTTPS

As we will see below, security was not "baked into" the web and has been awkwardly bolted on as an afterthought. Someone added a version of HTTP which was secured to at least some degree, which was named HTTPS. So this is also a URL:

```
https://www.mydomain.com/mydir/myfile.html
```

This assumes that the web server is configured to support HTTPS; not all of them are.

Web Client/Server

HTTP is a request/response protocol, which means that in practice there are web clients (any device running a web browser) and web servers (any server running web server software).

The World Wide Web is a collection of Internet hosts which are web servers and it is "browsed" by a variety of web clients running web browsers.

The servers are computers running web servers, in other words Internal hosts which are running HTTP server software.

Generally the client hardware is a personal computing device and the client software is a web browser such as Firefox, Chrome or Internet Explorer.

Web Page Layered Architecture

Here is an overview of the most basic web page request and retrieval:

1. User clicks on a link
2. Web Client browser makes an HTTP requests to a server
3. Web Server receives request
4. Web Server translates path to a file name or names
5. Web Server sends the file contents to the client
6. Web Client renders the contents for the user to see

HTML Example

Let us consider a very, very simple example.

Sample HTML Document

This is a sample HTML document:

```
<html>
  <head>
    <title>This is the page title</title>
  </head>
  <body>
    <h1>Header</h1>
    <p>A very simple web page (HTML document)</p>
  </body>
</html>
```

HTML is "structured" text in that a document has a pre-determined structure. An HTML document begins with "<html>" (or "<HTML>" if you prefer: HTML is case-insensitive) and ends with "</html>".

An HTML document has an optional header, which is found inside <head> and </head> tags (or the open and close head tags as some people think of them). In this case, the head has a title in it.

A HTML document has a mandatory body, which is found inside <body> and </body> tags. In this case, the body contains only a top level header found within the <h1> tags and a paragraph, which is found inside <p> and </p> tags.

Rendered Version

This is what that HTML looks like when my browser renders it: [3]

Header

A very simple web page (HTML document)

Real Life Complexities

The model given above is nice and simple but, of course, real life has gotten more complex. As the rather plain-looking image above demonstrates, the unvarnished web page is easy to create but not very pretty to look at.

Common Gateway Interface (CGI)

Relatively early in the web's history someone had the bright idea that a web resource might be an app instead of a file. The web server could run the app when it was requested and then treat the output of the app as an HTML document. Such HTML documents are called "dynamic" which leads to the alternative being called "static."

The definition of how an app is run by a web server is called the Common Gateway Interface (CGI). By convention, the apps were stored in a directory called "cgi-bin" for "the binaries which run CGI" because "binaries" is a term for runnable program files.

The CGI concept fits very neatly into the URL definition. Here is a URL for a program named "myprog":

```
http://www.mydomain.com/cgi-bin/myprog.cgi
```

It is common but not required to name the CGI apps with the extension ".cgi".

CGI opened up a vast array of possibilities and a large number of security problems. One of the possibilities is accessing data in databases, which is either a security boon (log in security) or a security bane (unauthorized database access).

Cascading Style Sheets (CSS)

People with information to publish were delighted by how easily and quickly and widely the web spread information. Graphic designers were dismayed by how drab that information appeared and how difficult it was to brand a web page with a distinctive look-and-feel. That need was addressed by the Cascading Style Sheet (CSS).

HTML web pages are made up "elements" such as paragraphs and headers and tables. These elements have attributes, such as font, font sizes, bold or not and others. The attributes determine how the elements are rendered by the browser (web client).

The style sheet concept is simple enough: the style sheet provides an override for the default rendered attributes of the elements of an HTML document. For example, style sheets allow one to specify the font size, color, etc for element such as a paragraph or a header.

The tricky part is that HTML style sheets "cascade" which means that style sheets can override the values in other style sheets. This makes CSS very powerful but also sometimes mind-bendingly complicated to follow and organize.

CSS also places a real burden on the rendering engine. In fact, when they first were released, CSS really dragged down the performance of browsers. At this point, computer hardware has cycles to burn so CSS is no longer a performance-killer.

CSS is still often mind-bendingly complicated to follow and organize.

Browser Scripting

Partway between static and dynamic content is the concept of browser scripting. Browser scripting is the practice of embedding some source code in the static HTML. That code will be executed in a limited environment by the browser.

The most common examples of browser scripting languages are JavaScript (somewhat aimed at Java programmers) and VBScript (heavily aimed at Visual Basic programmers).

There is a tension inherent in the browser scripting concept: the browser is local and privileged and presumed to be doing the user's bidding, but the script is remote and unknown and presumed to be potentially malicious (malware). Resolving this tension is mostly done by the fact that the browser is such a limited environment that we hope the browser scripting malware is not very harmful. This is not a great assumption. However, at this point, turning off scripting, which I do periodically as an experiment, makes many web sites ugly and some of them utterly unusable.

Java Applets

The limited environment afforded by browsers frustrated graphic designers and programmers alike. As it happens, there was a technology languishing in obscurity waiting to be an enhanced web page environment. That technology was Java.

Java is a C-derived, pseudo-compiled, pseudo-interpreted environment. The Java interpreter is a virtual machine, but a virtual version of a hardware platform which never existed. That Java VM is called "the Java Run Time Environment" (JRE).

Java was the brainchild of an engineer at Sun Microsystems, named Bill Joy. He had a vision of "write once, run everywhere" which would be accomplished by porting the JRE to as many platforms as possible. From cable top boxes to toaster.

Luckily, it did not come to toasters. Instead, the JRE was packaged up as a browser plug-in, as a browser extension. This allows web servers to serve up small Java apps, called "applets," which can extend web pages or even replace them.

The functionality that Java applets provide is impressive. The security holes that the JRE provides are terrifying. There is an entire subsystem which allows applets to access databases, which has the same pros and cons as CGI database access: log in support versus data theft.

The Net Effect

The net effect of browser scripting, CSS, CGI, Java and static HTML is mind-bogglingly complex. As long it all works, the effect is dazzling. When something along the long chain fails, finding and fixing the problem is often excruciatingly difficult. And so many organizational boundaries are crossed: the browser, the JRE, the scripting, the HTML, the CGI; sometimes all of them are owned by different organizations and Tech Support teams.

Chapter 16 End Notes

[1] In the beginning, some people called them "Universal Resource Indicators" or URIs, but they lost that popularity contest. There are still some references to "URIs" left on the web, so if you encounter one, it is just a synonym for URL. Some people also call them Uniform Resource Locators or Uniform Resource Indicators.

[2] https://www.cs.tut.fi/~jkorpela/ftpurl.html

[3] The process of turning an HTML document into a viewable image is called "rendering" and the software which does this job is called a "rendering engine."

Structured Query Language (SQL)

Who Created SQL?

Edgar F. Codd defined SQL because he had a vision of databases and database interactions and he wanted to make sure that implementations of his idea would not stray too far from this vision. [1]

Application Program Interface (API)

Apps often rely on services provided by system software. These supporting systems provide services which are common or privileged.

In order to access those services, the app needs an interface, a published way to call the service and to receive the output from that particular call. That published way is the Application Program Interface or API.

Common Functions

Common functions are provided by system software to encourage consistency and correctness. "Consistent" in this context means "does the same thing in the same situation that other apps do." "Correctness" in this context means "does not misbehave."

Different apps are consistent in their behavior if they all call the same support functions. Any app is correct (and reliable) if it call support functions which are thoroughly vetted and debugged.

Privileged Functions

Privileged functions, such as database access, need to be protected and controlled. The alternative is trusting all the apps to enforce the security policies consistently and correctly.

Report Generation

Back in the day, users only cared about one thing in the database realm: getting reports. Getting the right report with up-to-date information and without having to jump through too many hoops.

Before the Relational Database Management System (RDBMS) became so wildly popular, databases were an esoteric topic. The db admin was responsible for defining the "schema" (database structure) and for indexing (deciding which kinds of access would be fast and which would be slow).

Report programmers had to use whatever API the specific DBMS provided--assuming that the app development environment being used even had an API for that particular DBMS.

Since so much of the focus on databases was report generation, the relational model's tables map beautifully to the two dimensional paper page as well as the two dimensional web page.

Paper pages have lines and columns. The relational model's table has rows and columns. If one lays a table on a page with each table row becoming a line on the page, the result is a printable report.

An added benefit is that a data model based on a two-dimensional table made up rows of rows and columns is pretty easy for a non-programmer to understand.

With the advent of a data model people could relate to and an API that is so easy to use, there was no stopping the RDBMS.

SQL As API & UI

SQL is a linguistic interface to databases, which is a really odd thing that only seems normal now because we are so used to it. Before SQL there were various APIs for software and various UI methods and the two domains had nothing in common.

Now we have SQL which is accepted by the API, so the report programs have SQL statements in them, which means that db admins can help with debugging apps with embedded SQL statements even if the db admins cannot read or write the programming language in which the report is written.

We have visual programs which provide graphical user interfaces for users but a debugging mode which shows the SQL the UI creates, which means that the db admins can help support the user even if the db admins have no idea how to use the UI or the app providing the UI.

SQL Statements

The basic database operations are adding data, changing data, removing data and retrieving data. Each of these operations has an SQL statement ("command" if you prefer) as the API to make that request.

1. Adding data is done via the INSERT statement

2. Changing data is done via the UPDATE statement

3. Removing data is done via the DELETE statement

4. Retrieving data is done via the SELECT statement

The first three are database maintenance functions and are often restricted to db admins. Retrieval (also known as "read-only access") is open to a much wider circle of users.

SQL Select Statement

This section is intended to provide a basic overview of the Select statement so that if you encounter one in a report or during a debugging session with Tech Support, you will have some idea of what you are looking at.

The Select statement has these basic parts:

- The list of columns to be returned

- The tables from which to get those columns

- The conditions used to select the rows from which to get those columns

EXAMPLE ONE

Let us consider a simple example, a single table called "tab1," with three columns called "col1," "col2" and "col3".

The simplest case is taking all the columns from all the rows:

```
SELECT * FROM tab1
```

If you only want col1 as the data but only those rows for which col2 is "white":

```
SELECT col1 FROM tab1 WHERE col2='white'
```

Note that the column or columns returned by the SELECT statement are independent of the columns used in the WHERE clause. The above statement returns col1 but bases its selection on col2.

EXAMPLE TWO

For this example, we add another table, "tab2," which has four columns, "colA," "colB," "colC," "colD," and "col1". If we want a single SELECT statement to draw from multiple tables, we need to use the JOIN clause to specify both tables. There are simple JOIN clauses, which means that all rows of both tables are considered, and complex JOIN clauses, which means that there is some selection in the JOIN clause.

Although some implementations allow a simple JOIN to be done with a comma:

```
SELECT * FROM tab1, tab2
SELECT * FROM tab1 JOIN tab2
```

There are two common kinds of selection in the JOIN clause, but the second one of these is actually a version of the first.

The first kind of selection is the ON clause, which is a simplified WHERE clause by another name:

```
SELECT col1,colA FROM tab1 JOIN tab2 on(col2='WHITE')
```

If the schema has the same column in both tables, as ours does (col1 is common to both tables), then these two statements are equivalent:

```
SELECT * FROM tab1 JOIN tab2 on(tab1.col1=tab2.col1)
SELECT * FROM tab1 JOIN tab2 using(col1)
```

Chapter 17 End Notes

[1] Check out the uncharacteristically thin Wikipedia page https://en.wikipedia.org/wiki/Codd%27s_12_rules as a starting point.

CHAPTER 18   *Extensible Markup Language (XML)*   123

Extensible Markup Language (XML)

While all three of SGML, XML and HTML have "Markup Language" in their name, HTML is a markup langauge in name only. The other two, SGML and XML, are true markup languages. This means that they can define documents; in HTML, the document type definition (DTD) is already done.

What Is XML?

In theory, XML is a simpler-to-use, easier-to-process SGML. It turns out that defining document types is not that common a skill or that frequent a need.

In practice, mostly I see XML used as a cross-system data exchange mechanism. [1] In other words, XML document types are frequently used to create "documents" whose only purpose is to move data from one system into another.

Electronic Data Interchange (EDI)

Getting data into or out of a computer system is not a trifling matter and nothing to be sneezed at. I applaud the concept. I even admit that XML is okay at this job. My only objection is that the level of complexity and the amount of overhead involved in using XML is sometimes out of proportion to the benefit of using XML.

Data Models

Sadly, the level of effort in correctly and completely moving data between computer apps or computer systems is usually quite high. What usually determines how difficult the data interchange will be is the degree to which the two systems have the same "data model." A data model is the basic data organization used by the system. For example, I have seem many Electronic Medical Record (EMR) systems. Some are organized like this:

```
Encounter
    +---->Patient
    +---->Doctor
```

```
    +--->Start Date, End Date
    +--->Diagnosis
    +--->Procedures
```

Others are organized like this:

```
Patient
    +--->Encounter
            +--->Doctor
            +--->Start Date, End Date
            +--->Diagnosis
            +--->Procedures
```

Neither model is more correct or less correct; depending on what functions you want to perform and how your software is designed, one or other might be better for your specific purpose.

But moving data back and forth between the systems will be complicated by the fact that one system will want the data gathered up by Encounter and the other will want it gathered up by Patient. There is no simple "dump" that will be easy to export *and* easy to load into either system. (A dump is generally a simple text file generated to be machine-readable, not human-readable. Dumps are usually without much structure, which we call "flat" in computer jargon, hence the term "flat file.")

Optional History Lesson

Moving data from one computer system to another, what I call the "Export-Import Loop," used to be nearly impossible, mostly because very few producers of software had this as a goal. Why would anyone make it easy to take data out of their app, since the chief reason to export data was to migrate away from one app and onto another?

(Nowadays we all pay lip service to "inter-operability" which is a fancy way of saying "working together" but avoids sounding like a day-care poster. A certain degree of inter-operability is now assumed--of course your iPhone, your Windows PC and your TivO all work with the same network hardware. However, if you want a video call between your iPhone and your mother's Windows PC, you cannot use Apple's FaceTime, you have to use Skype instead, because it supports both platforms.)

Back in the day (the late 1970s and early 1980s), we often had to resort to using what I call "the Backup-Restore Loop" instead, picking apart backup files to get the data out and constructing back up files to get the data in. This was cumbersome, to say the least.

Then came the age of the Comma Separated Value (CSV) file. It was awesome for moving data back and forth between simple spreadsheets (unless you like formulas, in which case you were out of luck) and it was not bad for moving data back and forth between spreadsheets and databases, but the data models had to line up very closely or the difference had to be made up somewhere else.

If you wanted to move data between databases via CSV you often had to bridge the differences between data models with programming. If the programming was done on the way out from whatever source (to the CSV), that programming was an export process. If the programming was done on the way in (from the CSV to the database) that programming was an import process. If that programming happened after export but before import, it was called "middleware." [2]

XML Encodes Data Models

There was so much programming associated with CSVs: they were easy to understand but often hard to process. They were simple in structure but often the complexity had to go somewhere else--more CSVs, usually. So the market was ready for a "richer," more complex format which could represent a complex data model. In theory, being able to represent a complex data model would facilitate both exporting and importing. Ideally, much of the data exchange process could be automated, without any custom software; database management systems could be extended to easily translate their structures into XML structures and then fill those structures with their data, making export a push-button operation.

Similarly, database management systems could be extended to translate XML structures into database structures and then fill those structures with data from the XML file.

In practice, this is even mostly true. (There is software to operate on an XML as if it were a database, but that is beyond the scope of this book.)

XML Encodes Meta-Data

Meta-data is data about data. Common examples of meta-data include tagging an export file with time and date it was created, or the format used to create it, or the software and version used to create it.

Sometimes meta-data is needed to make sense of the data; for example, in order to process medical codes, you need to know which of the many possible medical coding schemes were used. To parse and store dates and date-times, you need to know how they are represented.

XML Is Here To Stay

XML is a textual way to represent data which is easy to process on a wide variety of computers and a wide variety of software environments.

XML's ability to encode both data and its data model means that it is a good choice for transferring data between systems.

XML's richness means that generalized software can display it; in fact, many browsers can render it as though it was HTML. XML's richness also means that it can actually be used as the back end of a DBMS.

Chapter 18 End Notes

[1] For which it seems like overkill to me.

[2] The fact that we have a name for it gives you some sense of how common it was.

Part VII

Conclusion

This part is a brief review of what I hope to have imparted and few reflections on the feedback I received from the pre-publication readers.

Conclusion

This chapter is a chance for me to reflect on what I hope you took away from reading this book and how I hope it will help you interact with IT.

Man Behind the Curtain

I hope that you have a sense of what lies behind the curtain, even if you do not know exactly what lies behind the curtain. This may help you make sense of explanations (and excuses) you get from Tech Support and may give you the confidence to ask questions when asking questions would be helpful.

Help IT Help You

I hope that you understand that you have some responsibility to ensure a satisfactory outcome to an IT encounter. Try to be precise. Try to be well-informed. Try to ready to answer some basic questions on what you want, or what you expected and what went wrong.

Reasonable Expectations

I hope you now have reasonable expectations of what IT can do and what Tech Support folks can accomplish. This should help you avoid at least some unsatisfying interactions with Tech Support folks.

Culture Clash

I hope you have a sense of what IT culture is like and how IT culture can clash with other corporate cultures. Knowing the cultural landscape may help you avoid issues which are misunderstandings and nothing more.

Empathy & Expertise

I hope you can see that Tech Support folks often lack empathy even as they have expertise. Specifically, Tech Support folks often lack the ability to understand what it is like to lack expertise; they can fall into the trap of assuming that everyone has (or should have) their knowledge and therefore users must be dimwits to ask the questions users ask.

Final Word

I am dismayed at how often users are dismayed or disappointed by their interactions with IT or Tech Support folks. I will be pleased with this book if it can help people avoid being dismayed or disappointed.

Index

A
Agile 96, 98
AIX 63
Application Software (apps) 28, 29, 36, 37, 38, 42, 43, 71, 73, 76, 85, 90, 91, 92, 93, 94, 114, 116, 118, 119, 123

B
Bluetooth 36
Boole 63
Booting 37
Bug 17, 26, 31, 56, 61, 89, 93, 97, 98, 99, 100, 101, 102, 103, 104, 105, 106, 107
Bug Report 106

C
Client/Server 38, 44, 92, 111
Cloud 22, 23, 56, 70, 74
Codd (father of relational databases) 118, 122
CSV 125

D
DBMS (Database Management System) 87, 119
DTD 123

Index

H
HTML (Hyper Text Markup Language) 87, 108, 109, 110, 111, 112, 113, 114, 115, 116, 117, 123, 126

I
IP 24, 49, 50, 51, 52, 53, 54, 55, 85, 110

J
JPEG 61

L
LAN 43, 45, 46, 51, 52
Linux 63

M
Mac 27, 30, 39, 49, 50, 54, 55, 56, 64, 65, 70, 73, 84, 90, 91, 116, 124
Middleware 125
MPEG 61

P
Patch 97
PC 21, 24, 27, 28, 29, 49, 50, 54, 85, 86, 124
PNG 61

R
Rendering Engine 115, 117

S

schema 119, 122
SGML (Standard Generalized Markup Language) 109, 110, 123
Skype 125
SQL 62, 63, 108, 118, 119, 120, 121, 122
sysadmin 54, 64, 65, 72, 73, 75, 76, 79, 80, 83, 85, 87, 89, 100
System Software (OS) 36, 37, 38, 43, 58, 63, 70

T

Therapist 17
Tool 29, 31, 44, 55, 68, 72, 77, 89, 90, 93, 106, 107

U

Unix 60, 61, 63, 86, 87
User Interface 35, 45, 77, 78, 99, 105, 106, 119, 120

V

Virtual Machine 70, 71, 72, 73, 74, 81, 83, 91, 92

W

WAN 45, 46, 51, 52, 53, 55, 56
Waterfall 97
Windows 17, 18, 38, 61, 85, 86, 87, 124
WLAN 45, 46, 51, 52, 55, 56

X

XML (Extended Markup Language) 108, 123, 124, 125, 126

www.ingramcontent.com/pod-product-compliance
Lightning Source LLC
Chambersburg PA
CBHW070143230526
45471CB00002B/502